On the Wings of Grace: A Story of Loss, Hope, and Redemption

On the Wings of Grace: A Story of Loss, Hope, and Redemption

By Fairlen Browning

On The Wings of Grace: A Story of Loss, Hope, and Redemption

All rights reserved © 2024 by Fairlen Browning
Published 2024
Clarksville, Tennessee

Disclaimer

This book is a work of non-fiction based on the life and memories of Fairlen Browning. Names, characters, places, and incidents are based on the memory, recollection, and research of author Fairlen Browning. This work depicts actual events in the author's life as truthfully as recollection permits and/or can be verified by research.

Occasionally, dialogue consistent with the character or nature of the person speaking has been supplemented. All persons within are actual individuals; there are no composite characters. The names of some individuals have been changed to respect their privacy. Any information based on actual persons, living or dead, businesses, companies, locales are intended to cause no harm to those that appear in this book.

On The Wings of Grace Publishing
ISBN: 979-8-218-43020-7

Foreword

The day I met Fairlen Browning changed my life.

It was December 7, 2012.

I was a reporter, and she was the keynote speaker at the Wings of Love event to honor murder victims at our local library.

I'm a self-proclaimed crybaby, and every year at the Wings of Love event, I break down crying while listening to the stories told by the honorees. That year, I really cried.

There stood Fairlen Browning in front of a large emotional crowd. Sophisticatedly dressed, poised, and proper. I remember a large evergreen tree adorned with lights illuminating her face, projecting a soft glow in the dimly lit room. The tree's branches were decked with hundreds of photo ornaments of homicide victims. Each of the victims' names was read aloud during the ceremony. Among those names was Fairlen's infant daughter, I'yanna. I was moved by Fairlen's bravery as she spoke with power about grief and her healing journey.

Wings of Love happened to fall on the anniversary of the day I'yanna Ellease Rawlins, was murdered by her father, who then took his own life. Fairlen shared her pain and healing with this group of people who knew all too well the devastation of losing a loved one in an act of violence.

When it was time to interview her, I was a hot mess of emotions. I had to give myself the *reporter pep talk* as I pulled it together so I could interview her. As I prepared to introduce myself, I was still choking back tears, attempting to remain professional and gather my thoughts accordingly. Several people lined up to greet Fairlen.

After patiently waiting, I walked up to her, shook her hand, and introduced myself. At the time, I hadn't known that I represented the same newspaper that had printed hurtful things after the death of her daughter. I'm actually happy I didn't know this at the time, as I'm sure it would have made me feel awkward and tense. Despite her experience with my employer, Fairlen was so friendly, kind, and willing to talk to me. We were instant friends, and she was such a down-to-earth, easy to talk to person. I knew I would never forget her.

I remember asking her how she could speak so courageously about something so tragic. She gracefully answered, and I'm paraphrasing, that God had helped her each time she spoke about the tragedy she'd experienced. She made it very clear that God was her strength, and she would not have made it through without him.

I told her in our first meeting, she was the strongest person I'd ever met, and I meant it - and still do to this day. She's the epitome of strength, perseverance, and faith. Fairlen and I formed a great professional friendship during my time as a reporter. I continued to cover stories about the local Parents of Murdered Children Chapter that she was a part of and the Children's Memorial Garden where I'yanna was the youngest murder victim honored there at that time.

Our conversations were always very down-to-earth, and we'd have a great time laughing, joking, and enjoying each other's company. She quickly became someone I admired, especially as a professional woman, community leader, speaker, and businesswoman. In one of our interviews, Fairlen said something that I would never forget, "I don't want anyone to forget I'yanna. I don't want I'yanna's death to be in vain." Those words forever remained with me.

Over a sushi lunch date years later, Fairlen asked me to do something that quickly reminded me of those words about I'yanna. She asked me to help write her and I'yanna's story. I was moved and very honored that she'd entrusted this special assignment to me. Our writing journey started quickly with interviews and long conversations. The journey was long, but there was a moment when we declared *it was finished*. When we looked back, it'd taken almost a decade to gather everything to tell her story.

Despite life continuing to interrupt and barge its way in, we never stopped telling I'yanna's story, we never gave up writing, and we forced our way through our life's obstacles, both facing our own trials and experiences in the process. To tell her complete story that time was necessary, and she said it was finished in "God's perfect timing."

During this writing journey, I was blessed to experience the birth of a daughter. Through the lens of motherhood, I wrote from a pivotal perspective that was essential to the writing of Fairlen and I'yanna's story. Watching Fairlen experience motherhood to a daughter again with Hannah was also an experience that added to the full circle story of motherhood, love, loss and rising beyond obstacles.

This is Fairlen's story that she has worked tirelessly to share with the world.

Dedication

To my children Asha, Hannah, and I'yanna.
My love for you is eternal.

I want others to know that there is hope after tragedy and that you can heal and progress in life without losing the memory of your loved one. - Fairlen Browning

Chapter 1

The Mission
Spring 2007

Adrian whipped his red Mercury Montego into the Shell gas station parking lot and came to an abrupt stop at the gas pump.

He was in a rush.

The mood was tense inside the car as I sat with my arms folded across my chest.

It was quiet.

I could feel his irritation radiating as he drove quickly through town speeding to complete the mission. I gently held my stomach. I felt sick.

We were running late and needed to be on the highway already, but the car's gas needle was hugging "E" and stopping for gas seemed to make the tension and my dreaded anticipation worse.

Adrian turned the car off, unbuckled the seatbelt, and opened the car door. The car's annoying chime urged him to get out. I was instinctively holding my breath, and my chest felt extremely heavy.

"Aye... you want anything?" Adrian asked not looking in my direction.

"Naw. I'm good," I said.

In that second, I could see, feel, and inhale his disappointment, irritation, and anger all contained in the quiet, laidback, calm man that he was. It was like he was speaking to me through a clenched jaw but refusing to show any pain.

He knew. I knew.

This man's demeanor was the opposite of all the times we'd gone to doctor's offices in the past for prenatal care. Thinking back, he'd been so supportive and cared for me through a miscarriage and the birth of our son. But this pregnancy was different and there was no compassion for me or the unborn child I was carrying. What we were experiencing was a foreign matter to us both.

Ironically, this strain to even speak was us fighting for us. This sacrifice I was about to make was proof that I was willing to risk it all to make my marriage to Adrian work.

Adrian slammed the door as he got out of the car.

I exhaled.

At that moment, I realized he hated the whole thing just as much as I hated it. Yet, it was an unspoken truth that his empathy was extremely short when it came to me. I felt he thought I deserved the pain that lay ahead for me just 60 miles up the road at a Nashville abortion clinic.

Adrian's return from Iraq had been just two days before his abortion ultimatum. His homecoming had been such a bittersweet event. In just five short days, everything about our plan to halt our pending divorce and start over had blown up in my face, changing and destroying our dreams of reconciliation.

I'd recently found out I was pregnant and knew when he returned from deployment, I couldn't keep this a secret. I'd thought about making him think he got me pregnant upon his return, but he's smarter than that. The math would not have been mathin'. Besides, I hated those girls on daytime TV shows like *Maury* or *Jerry Springer* trying to put a baby on a guy and knowing it's not his. For the first time, I could understand their desperation.

Our plan was perfect. Upon his return from an 18-month deployment we were supposed to have a fresh start. We'd opened ourselves up and bore our souls to each other, confessing our indiscretions, and were ready to take on our vows anew.

I'd told him I'd cheated, and he'd admitted he'd stepped outside the marriage, too. I was paying for my brokenness and the baby that was growing in my womb would be a casualty of the war we were fighting to reconcile.

He'd made himself perfectly clear. He was willing to do anything to fix us; anything, except raise another man's baby.

Point. Blank. Period.

And for him, the solution was simple. I needed to get an abortion immediately. He had an easy plan to put our pieces back together. He would pay for my abortion, put in orders to be stationed at a post far away from the Fort Campbell/Clarksville area, and with our son, AJ, we'd start over. That was the plan, and if I wanted my family to work, I'd put on my big girl panties and get it done so we could move forward.

I'd committed the ultimate military spouse sin and had an affair while Adrian was deployed to Iraq. Loneliness, resentment, and giving in to my fleshly desires were at the core of my indiscretions. I didn't make excuses and chose accountability. He hadn't been perfect in our marriage either, but I was the one who had proof of my infidelity. I wanted to make it work and I wanted to be a family. I accepted his plan and was committed to following through with it.

My brain was running a million miles a minute. I felt myself slip into my quiet, strong place. This was a very familiar place for me as I'd been there so many times in my life as I faced many tough situations. I never let anyone know they were getting to me, and it allowed me to stand tall and face obstacles without crumbling. I'd pray, close my feelings off, and get into business mode to deal with whatever was on the other side of life's door.

On this day, I found it hard to pray. What was I going to say? *God, please help me have strength as I go abort my child?* Yeah. I couldn't bring myself to ask God for anything like that.

I had to be content with leaning on my ability to stay strong. Whether it was being bullied in school due to being the big girl, rejection from my father, or my mother's tough love, I knew how to retreat to my safe space and remain strong when faced with a struggle. I was 24 years old, and I knew I had much more life and love to give. I knew I'd get through this, and we'd be alright.

The little voice in my head was screaming relentlessly, taunting me. *I was on my way to get an abortion. I was on my way to kill my baby.* Being a mom was a huge priority in my life and I adored my son. I had hoped Adrian could accept this baby growing in me, but that was wishful thinking.

Abortion.

It's crazy because anytime I'd see one of those sidewalk rallies with the abortion-hating groups, I'd quickly look away from the graphic mangled, bloody fetuses on the posters and think, *How could anyone do that to their child?* But here I was about to do *that* to my unborn child. I knew why I was doing it. I just didn't know how I could really go through with it.

My appointment was at 1:30 p.m. It was 12:45 p.m. I knew Adrian would turn his music up, tear down I-24, and have us in that doctor's office somehow with 10 minutes to spare. Then I'd be there, bright lights, and cold steel instruments waiting for me. I imagined myself, laying on my back, feet in stirrups as a doctor ripped, tore, vacuumed, scrapped, and devastated my soul.

I pictured myself weeping uncontrollably in pain and shame. I imagined Adrian across the room staring out the window listening, waiting, not holding my hand or caring. Then I imagined a sympathetic nurse watching as tears rolled down my cheeks. I could only assume that I'd feel everything in my being and body collapsing as that baby left my body. I imagined myself bleeding profusely, crippled in pain knowing a part of who I was would emotionally and morally perish from this sacrifice I was making for my marriage.

I'd always been taught that abortion was wrong in God's eyes. Anna, my mom, raised all three of her girls in the church, and I'd heard the sermons and knew all too well how God felt about it. I agreed with the idea of the sanctity of life, but with a self-destructing finality, I'd turned a blind eye to my faith. I had to.

I ended the graphic daydream with Adrian looking at me after it was all over. Satisfaction in his eyes as he helped me to the car as I reeled in pain, barely walking as I bore my self-inflicted destruction. Maybe I'd watched too many movies or heard too many stories from girls who'd had abortions in high school. Either way, some horrible version of this daydream was about to be my reality.

Would he really be happy? I honestly thought he would be content, and it would even the score so to speak. I knew he wanted his family, and he could move past his hurt if there were not a constant reminder present.

Adrian was a loving man, somewhat hardened by the demands of the military, but his weak spot was me, and I knew it. Knowing that I had his heart made me both powerful in fulfilling my duties as a wife and weak to everything inside me. This duality worked counter to what I knew was right.

I could always see calamity before it happened. Haunted by premonitions of self-destruction. Even when I knew I was sabotaging and knew there was a right and wrong decision, my youth and lack of wisdom led me to follow my heart on decisions I knew might lead to having it broken. I knew I was about to make the wrong decision, but it didn't stop me from making it.

Chapter 2

18 Years Young
Spring 2000

When I met Adrian, I was young, impressionable with the thoughts and whims of a young woman trying to be grown. As the oldest of my sisters, Gabby and Monica, I had maturity. I helped raise them and ran the household as my single mom, Anna, worked tirelessly to provide for us.

Something happens to a girl the year before she turns 18. It's like this fire awakens in her bones and she no longer thinks logically. All her good sense goes to the wind, and she can hear nothing but the dreams and what-ifs that life presents. It's the feeling of being a legal adult but lacking the wisdom and knowledge to truly hold that title of adult. That was definitely me, but I also knew I wanted to be a businesswoman one day and had dreams and aspirations. I was an intelligent young lady, but my inexperience led to me not making the wisest choices at times.

I was the kind of girl that made friends easily and could work a room with charisma and charm. I was known for being quick-witted and having a big sense of humor. My sarcasm wasn't mean-spirited, but I could dish it, and I could take it. I've always had a big laugh and loved to create a warm environment, establish camaraderie, and hold deep conversations.

I also have always been a passionate person with deep emotions. When I feel deeply about something it's apparent in how I think, speak, and act. Love has always been something I felt deeply about. I've always been a bit of a hopeless romantic and loved big.

I was also *a big girl*, but I was confident because I felt my personality compensated for my size even though I know that doesn't sound great. I've always wanted people to see beyond my exterior and just love me for me. However, externally I always kept myself looking, feeling, and smelling good. My mom taught us how to carry ourselves with dignity and enforced being clean.

And even yet, while I was confident in myself, it didn't stop some insecurities about my weight from creeping in from time to time. There was a big difference between being plus sized versus being attractively *thick* during that time. And even in the early 2000s being plus-sized had not yet reached its, somewhat, acceptance as it does now. However, I guess, being classified as the typical light-skinned girl with a good grade of hair, as the old folks used to say, was the balance to distract from the weight. Yet, I understood despite those things I was not a bad-looking woman and that I was completely confident in how I carried myself like a lady.

It was 2000, or Y2K, as the year was popularly called. I was 17 years old and, on my way, to being a senior at Manhattan High School in Manhattan, Kansas. It had been home for the past five years and I had finally acclimated to this new culture. To some, I was a bit exotic. Mostly because I was from Mississippi and my distinct southern drawl was very noticeable. Also, I didn't look like anyone in the area, everyone immediately noticed the Creole in me.

It was law in our house to look your best and always be neat and clean. Momma didn't raise any slouchy girls, and that's why I kept a new set of French tip acrylics and rarely missed my bi-weekly appointments at the hair salon. She also ran a tight, clean ship in our home. Our cleaning soundtrack was filled with '90s R&B or gospel every Saturday and you could smell the bleach and Pine-Sol from the front porch. I believe it was these Saturday rituals and Momma's demands where my obsessive-compulsive tendencies about cleaning were birthed. My sisters and I knew the rules and what was required of us when we wanted anything from Momma. However, we knew how to work around them when we needed to in order to get what we wanted.

I spent my late summer vacation nights on AOL dial-up using the family computer. Back then the only way to get online was through telephone dial-up. Since the house phone line was rarely in use we had free rein on the Internet.

Internet Explorer, chat rooms, e-mail, and messenger apps were new to our generation, and we began to quickly absorb and take on advancing technology as part of our daily lives. Oh, what a time to be alive as we enjoyed the excitement of exploring what would later be called social media and communicating online. It was fun hiding behind a screen and chatting with random people. Me and my sisters would laugh and cut up as we browsed the online dating chat rooms for all the singles in the area, rating their looks, and typing in randomness in chat rooms.

A/S/L (Age, Sex, Location) ... 25, F, California...Type, type, type. Giggle, giggle, giggle.

Like many girls my age, I spent many nights downloading free music onto my blank CDs and introducing all kinds of viruses on our family computer. It was on BlackPlanet.com where I found someone real who would change my life.

BlackPlanet.com was an early social network for Black singles to meet and mingle. It was much like MySpace.com, and existed years before there was Facebook, Instagram, Snapchat, Twitter (now called X), or TikTok. It was the ground zero of social media, but innovative and exciting for Millennials.

Among the many new faces in this exciting cyberspace, a man named Adrian caught my eye, and I caught his. Adrian was 20 years old. He was a soldier stationed nearby at Fort Riley and was from the Virgin Islands. What started as a few messages became long chat conversations and a combustion of chemistry. He was easy to talk to and seemed honest and genuine. I couldn't stop smiling as we sent messages back and forth, flirting, and connecting through a computer screen. It was literally a computer love.

Despite my mother's warnings about the World Wide Web and sexual predators, I gave him my phone number, and we soon found ourselves talking all the time. He was a real person, not a catfish, as it would be later termed. I'd just got my first cell phone–a silver Nokia flip phone–and was ecstatic learning to text and be in touch with my friends wherever I went. Cell phones were still a luxury and not a necessity in 2000, especially for teenagers.

I remember fawning over Adrian's deep accent, it was to die for, and I couldn't wait to hear it again each time we'd get off the phone. As different as we were, it was such a unique, exciting time every time we talked. He was so interesting. Because of my outgoing and talkative nature, I'd ask him all kinds of crazy questions, and he didn't mind. I think that is what also attracted him to me. I wasn't afraid to be vocal. I was always excited to learn more about him. Adrian was the opposite of me. He was laid-back and super chill – it truly appeared that opposites attracted.

I was immediately impressed by Adrian, which was an accomplishment for him, as impressing me was not an easy thing to do. At just 20 years old, he was far more mature than any man his age or any man that I'd known. He was always about his grown-man business. I think I was more impressed that he was nothing like the boys in high school who were immature, wore super baggy clothes, and had no real-life goals.

I'd engaged Adrian and kept in contact with him despite being in a long-term relationship with a boy at school named Calvin. Calvin was a PK, a preacher's kid, and we'd dated from eighth grade until I met Adrian. Calvin was a "good" guy. I often went to his family's home for Bible study and prayer.

Preachers' kids get the reputation for being the worst, especially in youth. Although church kids, Calvin and I were not as holy as everyone thought. However, my mom felt comfortable with Calvin only because his family was in church, and because she'd raised us in church. So naturally, she pushed me toward being with him, and at the time, I didn't think it was such a bad idea.

Calvin and I had a lot in common. We were good kids experimenting with life, and we were friends but knew how to navigate the waters of the church and the world. I learned early that the commonality of the church was important to me, and despite later breaking up, Calvin taught me how important it was to be evenly yoked in the Lord with another person.

I always loved God and enjoyed my connection with God even at a young age. But going through the troubled waters of youth without a lot of direction or supervision, I often followed my heart and went against my better moral judgment. It would be years before I would focus more on my walk with God.

My heart led me to Adrian, and I made a complete 180-degree turn from a preacher's kid to a worldly man. Adrian didn't even know if he believed in God and religion was a taboo subject that he'd rather not discuss even when I tried to talk about my church or religious activities. He'd say he wasn't "into all that stuff." Despite that, I still was attracted to Adrian because he was nice to me. He didn't seem too bad, and it soon didn't matter to me his religious views. After some time of talking over the phone and the Internet, our computer love turned to real-life interactions.

Fort Riley to Manhattan was less than 15 miles away. When we found out how close we were there was no keeping us apart. Unbeknownst to my mom, I started dating Adrian and seeing him frequently.

The first time we met in person we immediately confirmed our magnetic attraction for one another that we were feeling over the phone. He was handsome, tall, and attentive and he made me smile. It was like he saw my heart, my struggle, my accomplishments. He didn't just focus on outer appearance but told me I was smart and that he admired that.

As a young woman, I was attracted to the way he carried himself, and from day one, he took care of me without me asking for it. He was an *open your door, hold your umbrella, walk on the left side of the sidewalk* type of dude, and I loved all of the queen treatment. He got paid twice a month and he would make sure I had what I needed. He spoiled me even before we were officially dating. All I had to do was ask, and the answer was always yes.

At 17, it was appealing to and fulfilling my desire to be taken care of, adored, and held in high esteem by a man. A man had never shown me what real love was. I didn't really have a relationship with my father, as I knew him by name only and never in a more intimate way. At the time, I didn't understand how my father's physical absence would affect me and create a void in my life.

Adrian was a kind-hearted man. He was easy to talk to and was very open to talking about deep things with me. Despite our physical attraction to one another, he was really my friend. Although we hadn't known each other for a long time, I quickly grew to trust him. The innocence of youth had me falling so hard for him and falling fast. I was smitten!

We'd soon become intimate, and on several occasions, I'd sneak off to be with him. I had become sexually active and couldn't stop myself from being with him. Adrian made me feel safe, wanted, and needed. As our relationship progressed, I knew I wanted to marry him. He had my nose wide open, as the old folks would say.

Adrian was the first guy since Calvin I brought home to meet Momma. This was a huge deal because Anna did not play, and she had good reason not to. Momma had been a teen mom and drilled into her three girls the hardships she'd faced raising us alone. We were not supposed to repeat her mistakes. Anna's girls were not going to be out there *hoein' in the streets* and become single teen moms. She would drill us constantly about our sexual activities. She used outrageous methods of ensuring our purity by *checking us* and asking embarrassing questions. My mom was obsessed with our sexual lives. This obsession led me to being sorely afraid of the wrath I thought I'd face if my mom ever found out that I wasn't a virgin anymore. Looking back, I understand why Momma was like that. It wasn't as much about the sex but more about trying to protect us from men.

But her protection was never going to be enough for the void in my life. I was searching for something else. I wanted to be loved and wanted. There was a feeling I was chasing. Adrian fulfilled that early on in our relationship, but it would soon fade as the relationship progressed. Adrian was a true-to-heart military man, and I'd soon be riding in the backseat as military life was going always to be in the front seat with Adrian.

As I entered my senior year in the fall, Adrian got orders to deploy to Korea. He reassured me that despite him leaving, our relationship wouldn't change, and when he returned from deployment, he wanted to marry me. While foreign to me, the thought of marriage felt secure and safe. Most of the women in my family had never been married, so the idea of marriage soon became a goal that I wanted to achieve. I'd soon dream of having a big house, children, a white picket fence, a dog, a good job, and nice cars. I wanted love and romance... the works. I believed I could have it with Adrian. I knew I could circumnavigate my generational curses.

Just as all my life seemed to take off, my carelessness and my youth sucker punched me. As I geared up for my senior year in high school, life came crashing down just as quickly as I'd planned how perfect it could be.

Chapter 3

My Mother's Mistake

My period was late.

I was panicking but had also convinced myself nothing was wrong. It would show up. It was just stress.

Life couldn't be this cruel.

I was living life carefree and happy. It was the first semester of my senior year of high school, and graduation was in sight. I was excited. Things were going well with Adrian, and we were as close as ever. We had been spending all of our available time together. When I wasn't at school or when he wasn't working, we were together. I was nervous about his deployment and didn't want him to leave. I was in love with this man, so much so I'd sneak off to be with him in his barracks and made love to him every night I had the chance.

I hadn't told him about my period being late because I desperately hoped that it would magically show up. But soon, I knew I had to face the inevitable; deep down, I knew I was pregnant, but I was in denial. One day I started experiencing headaches and cramping so bad that I knew I had to take a pregnancy test.

I remember sneaking off to get a pregnancy test. I rushed home and quickly locked myself in the bathroom. I ripped open the test box and pulled out the test from the foil wrapper, sat on the toilet, peed on the stick, and then sat it on the sink. I barely wanted to look at it, but I knew I had to face the truth. I picked up the pregnancy stick. It was one of the fancy new digital sticks that didn't have lines but would read "pregnant" or "not pregnant" in the little white window of the stick.

"Pregnant."

I was mortified. I was numb and could not believe I was pregnant. I knew I had to tell Adrian as soon as possible. I remember the evening that I invited him over it was a very warm day. We were sitting on the porch, and I was so nervous.

I could barely look him in the eyes. I was barely able to form the words, I quietly whispered, "I need to tell you something."

My stomach was in knots. Would he freak out? Would he be upset? I didn't know. I was terrified and confused. I couldn't believe I was pregnant. How could this happen to me? I mean, I knew how, but why me?

I took a deep breath and blurted it out. "I'm pregnant!"

Adrian turned to me, and his face lit up. "Really!?"

Was he excited? For a moment I felt a wave of relief wash over me. He was happy. It felt like I had an ally immediately. Then I remember this was not good news for me. I was still in high school with a mother who was going to literally beat the *yella'* off me for having a baby, not only as a teen and out of wedlock, but repeating her mistake.

I told Adrian all my worries and concerns. He was immediately supportive and reassured me he would take care of me, and we would get through it together. I remember being in tears thinking my life was ending before it began. He'd hugged me and promised to help me tell my mom when the time was right.

The one thing Momma drilled in me not to do, I did. I'd repeated the generational curse by throwing caution to the wind, gambling with my life by taking no birth control and having no care. Thinking I knew what I was doing and that I was grown. I was blinded by love and passion. I was chasing high moments that felt good and made me feel loved. Although I was stressed and overwhelmed, Adrian's reassurance put me at ease. It would be okay. I would be okay. We'd get married, be a family, we'd be okay.

My mom had been mothering since she was a kid. Everyone who knew her called her Momma Anna. My mom raised me and my two sisters, Gabrielle "Gabby" and Monica, with a few key principles: always stick together, stick up for each other, and take care of each other because we were all we had. She constantly reminded us to keep our home clean because cleanliness was next to godliness and not to repeat her mistakes with men - like having a baby as a teenager and becoming a single mother. Momma was always going to share with us what she deemed as mistakes in detail to ensure we "got it." She'd threatened us and instilled the fear of God in us not to adopt the hardships that had put her life on a trajectory to struggle most of her life in loneliness.

Momma didn't want us to be among those who *lived off of the system*, so she was very adamant about teaching us to work for what we wanted in life and was huge on ensuring we had an education. Even though she worked all the time, she still made time to be there for all of our school functions and would often pop up in the classroom. To this day, I still don't know how she did all that she did. It wasn't until I was an adult, that I learned that we were among the poor working class. She made it look easy. My sisters and I never wanted for anything. Our clothing was always well put together, we always had clean white shoes, and meals were never missed. But looking back at it I realized Momma made many sacrifices so that we could always look presentable. I remember seeing my mom sew her underwear back together, while we were walking around with new clothes. She taught me the meaning of sacrificial love. The love my mother had for me and all she poured into me at 17 years old was amazing. She was a child herself but had to grow up quickly upon learning that she was pregnant.

I couldn't appreciate her story until I was in those same 17-year-old shoes. To know that I would break my mother's heart broke my heart. I could now appreciate the magnitude of the hopes and dreams she had poured into her children. Us. Me.

We were supposed to be smarter than her. Our choices were supposed to be wiser because she'd taken the time to educate us on what not to do. My mother had spoken to us so much about all her mistakes that I could recite them effortlessly without even thinking. While I believe no child is a mistake, I now understood how I, too, was a product of what she considered to be a stream of bad decisions. But I didn't listen.

This is how Momma would always tell her story. She was the big girl, and this very attractive married man named Bobby liked her. She believed and trusted in his empty words and promises. She was careless. She was sneaking behind her mom's back. Then the pregnancy, the fear, the pain of childbirth, the loneliness, the struggle. As the oldest daughter, I had lived all the hardships with her. I stood with her as she faced life as a single teen mom. I knew it all by heart because I witnessed it.

Yet somehow, I naively thought it could never be me. Yet, there I was a replica of my mom. I was so embarrassed and ashamed of myself. I remember not wanting my sisters to know anything about my pregnancy. I was supposed to be their example, and ironically, I would find myself drilling into them as my mom drilled into us.

My thoughts were everywhere. I convinced myself I could do this teen pregnancy situation differently. I knew I could. Although his deployment to Korea was in a couple of weeks, I knew he wouldn't leave me and our child to struggle.

I was young and scared. The what-ifs consumed every waking hour. I couldn't concentrate. For me, it was a whirlwind, teenage love affair full of grown-up issues. What weighed the most on me was how would I tell my momma I was pregnant.

Momma liked Adrian after meeting him for the first time. As strict as my mom was, I was surprised that she was comfortable with me dating him. She had even allowed him to come hang out in our home. Of course, there were restrictions like no doors were to be closed, he was not allowed in my bedroom, and we had to have a chaperone whenever we went out. Usually Gabby or Monica, but that didn't make a difference because they were on my side. When my mom was around, of course, there was no such thing as alone time with each other. Obviously, we made up for that when we snuck around. Despite all that, the fact that she genuinely liked him meant everything to me. Momma bragged to everyone about how respectful Adrian was and how he could hold an intelligent conversation with her. She loved that he was a serviceman and could pay his bills and do his laundry at his age.

 This was all about to change the moment I told her we'd been having sex and he'd gotten me pregnant. I'd betrayed her trust. I feared that my pregnancy would smother all the good about him in my family's eyes. I know that should've been the least of my worries, but I cared about Adrian and feared this would ruin my mom's fond thoughts of him.

We continued to prolong telling my mother about my pregnancy, but Adrian knew that I needed prenatal healthcare.

He wanted me to take care of myself and make sure the baby and I were well. After searching on the Internet, I found a clinic that accepted pregnant minors without parental consent. I skipped school and Adrian drove me to the clinic. He was so reassuring and present. Although I already knew I was pregnant, at the doctor's office they had to take another test to confirm their records.

While I sat in fear, he was unabashedly excited about his first child. Adrian was so ready to be a dad. While I worried about being alone with a child, he wasn't worried at all. He understood what came with military life and their families: deployments, pregnancies, and marriage. I wasn't sure I understood that life, let alone was completely ready for it. But I was going to find out quickly.

At the clinic, we were waiting for the results. For some reason, it was torture for me. I think I was secretly hoping that they would come back with a negative test and tell me that I was just experiencing a hormonal fluke that disrupted my cycle. However, when the nurse came back with the results, she explained my urinalysis pregnancy test came back as a partial positive.

Adrian and I were obviously confused. What the heck was a partial positive? I thought to myself, I'm either pregnant or I'm not. However, the doctor quickly explained that I needed to come back in a couple of days to allow my HCG (the pregnancy hormone) levels to increase. I still was very early in my pregnancy, but the doctor stated that based on how far along I was my HCG levels should have been higher. Also, the doctor stated he wanted to make sure I wasn't having a tubal, or ectopic, pregnancy. I didn't understand what any of this meant, and it only pushed me further into anxiety about it all. I was terrified with what was going on inside my body. It was two days of torture as I walked around my mother's home with this burdening secret. I was trying to stay strong and attempted to be my normal chipper self with the world on my shoulders.

Two days later, I skipped school again and Adrian drove me back to the doctor for a second test. We were both nervous but were ready for an answer. We found ourselves in utter shock when the test came back again as a partial positive. My HCG levels had not increased enough to have a healthy or likely pregnancy, the doctor explained. He suspected that I most likely was having a tubal pregnancy. I was told I may need a surgical procedure called a dilatation and curettage, or D&C, as it was commonly known as, to remove the fetus if my body didn't naturally miscarry on its own.

This was the worst position to be in. I was not ready to tell Momma, but we had to. Adrian and I wanted to wait it out, but we knew we didn't have time. When the doctor first explained that while he didn't have to inform my mother I was pregnant, she did need to be informed if I was going to have the surgery. So having the D&C quietly was completely out of the question.

Then the doctor further went on to explain that time was of the essence. I could be facing a more serious medical emergency if the pregnancy wasn't viable, and my body didn't naturally miscarry. I didn't want to put myself in medical danger and neither did Adrian. We both knew there was no way around it and no more waiting. Reluctantly, we decided to tell Momma that weekend. My heart sank, and my anxiety rose even more. I was worried about everything. Worried about having a miscarriage. Worried about needing surgery. Worried that my mom would hate me and Adrian.

My emotions swirled. I was crushed, confused, elated, terrified, and guilt-ridden for my elation all at the same time. I wanted my baby, but I also didn't want to be a teen mom either. I'd heard about girls my age speaking about getting abortions. Ironically, that never entered my mind because, in my family, abortions were never an option. We did not believe in it and felt it was a sin before God. If I was going to have a baby, I wanted my baby to be alive and healthy. Yet, I wasn't prepared to be a mom at this young age. It was a complex set of emotions, but I grieved the loss of life within me, yet at the same time was relieved.

I went over and over in my head about how we were going to relay the news to Momma. I thought that the majority chance of the pregnancy ending in miscarriage would soften the blow and she'd have mercy on me. It was a horrible self-preserving thought, but in all my fear it made sense in the moment.

I'd been lying to her for months. When I first told her about Adrian, she asked me straight up if I had been having sex with him or anyone else. I'd emphatically told her no and said I was still a virgin. But I knew I'd been wilding out with Adrian since we met.

The Saturday after my last doctor's appointment, I asked if Adrian could come over. When he arrived, I called my mother to the living room and told her we needed to talk to her. As she watched us sitting on the couch, I could tell she knew immediately, but she didn't say anything. She waited for our confession. Her demeanor became defensive. Her gaze was accusatory. She wouldn't sit down. She stood with her arms crossed.

"What's going on?" She asked.

I didn't mince words. I took a deep breath, and I shot it straight. "Momma, I'm pregnant and I may be having a miscarriage and need surgery soon."

Just like that. All in one run-on sentence and one breath. I kept my eyes steady on her. The silence was deafening. I could see her processing the words as her face changed. I braced myself for what was coming.

My mom is one of those people whose face shows her emotions immediately. My mother's face dropped, and her eyes became large and outraged as she yelled, "What!?" I'd imagine that she was going through the same knowing yet in denial that I went through when I first realized I was pregnant. Her arms began flailing as she spoke loudly and gestured forcefully. Her voice rose quickly with emotion as she screamed at me, "Fairlen, are you (expletive) serious!?"

Momma was not a crier. She was fierce and strong and raised us in what she called the "old school" way. She was furious, and profanity flowed from her mouth like a wide-open faucet. As I watched her move toward me in rage, I thought she was going to beat me down and choke me out. Her hands struck the air with emphasis with every word she yelled. She let it all out, unleashing the fury of a million Black mommas on me and Adrian.

She cursed us both clean out, calling us everything but a child of God. I was embarrassed. She was outraged and hurt. It honestly crushed me to see her so disappointed in me. How could I do the very thing she'd drilled into me not to do? I stayed quiet. I knew not to try and justify anything or even speak.

Adrian sat next to me also quiet. We both let her have the moment. I'd told him about my mom, but he'd always seen the funny, happy side of her. He'd never heard her yell this loud or seen her angry.

Momma's petite 5'5 stature paced the floor. Her ponytail whipped as she became more infuriated and irate. She was not one to play with. She was stout and I believe could knock someone out in one punch.

"You think you're slick, sneaking around my (expletive) back, don't you lil' girl?!" She said pointing at me. "Lying to my (expletive) face when I do everything for you!!! You think you a woman!? Opening your legs to this man who don't owe you nothing. You stupid!"

My face turned hot and red, but I tried not to let my mom see me crumble from disappointing her. I knew I failed her. Her dreams and goals for me had been obliterated at that moment.

She disappeared into her room and then reappeared randomly and started talking to herself. "They not going to play me like I'm a (expletive) fool!"

Adrian and I glanced at each other without a word and our eyes said, "Yeah she's going off." She put on her shoes, grabbed her keys, and told Adrian to bring his "(expletive, expletive)" and get in the car. "You stay!" She told me as I stood up.

The look she shot me sent chills down my spine. If looks could kill I was surely dead. Adrian towered over my mom and respectfully followed her out the door.

"What in the world was she going to do?" I wondered aloud.

I ran to the window and watched as Adrian got into Momma's car, and she sped off. I was pacing and panicking.

Where were they going? Is she going to kill him? What is happening?

I texted Adrian's phone... *What is going on? Where are y'all going?*

He texted me back with about seven question marks and replied, *I don't know, but she's really mad!*

I was sick to my stomach and then it all fell on me. I spent an unknown amount of time crying and praying. Begging for forgiveness and asking for mercy. I asked God for a way out or an answer. Just something to ease me in the moment.

"God, what had I done? Was this punishment? Why didn't I listen to Momma? I'd ruined everything." I prayed earnestly.

I waited nervously, staring at my cell phone to make sure I didn't miss Adrian's text message. What was Momma saying or doing to him? When Momma finally came back to the house the sun was setting. It'd been almost two hours. Adrian wasn't with her.

I didn't dare run and look out the window, but I heard his car door shut and he drove off. My mom looked exhausted and tired. She walked through the living room, slammed her keys on the table, and turned around and just stared at me.

I was looking back at her, my face no longer able to hold back letting her see me break.

"Momma, I'm sorry," I said, weeping.

When I looked closer at her, I saw the small puffs under her eyes. She'd been crying too, and she was not a crier. I knew she was hurt. I felt terrible.

She'd already cursed Adrian and me out from A to Z, and she was lost for words. She shook her head and walked to her room, slamming the door. The silence cut through the lingering tension in the air, and in that moment, I truly think her disappointment hurt worse than anything.

That night, I quietly talked on the phone to Adrian from my bedroom, almost whispering.

"You OK?" I asked him quietly.

"Yeah... I'm good," he said, his accent thick as usual.

"Where'd you go?" I asked.

"I don't know where we was goin'!" He said.

"What was she saying?" I asked, knowing she was most likely talking crazy to him.

Adrian explained how my mom drove him far out of the city limits to some unknown lake. She parked the car and looked at him dead in the eyes and threatened his life. She told him if he thought he was going to get me pregnant, go off to Korea, and leave me and this baby to fend for ourselves she had something coming for him.

"What!?" I said in disbelief as he further explained how she told him she had brothers who would put him in that lake and no one would ever find his body if he hurt me in any way.

My uncles weren't thugs or mobsters who would even do that. But somehow, I knew Momma was dead serious with her threats. She would have him hurt because she did not play about her three daughters.

"Then she asked to see my social security card," Adrian said. "Had me write down my information and everything."

"Ooooh, nooo!" I whispered, shaking my head and trying not to laugh. My mom did not play. "She did not!" I softly whispered in the phone.

"Yeah, man. I was telling her I'm not no bum. I'd never leave you to take care of our child alone and I promised her I'd take care of you," he said. "We don't even know if you are going to have a baby."

His voice trailed off and it got quiet. We hadn't even had a chance to deal with the fact that my pregnancy was ending in a miscarriage. The disappointment in his voice broke my heart.

"I know," I said, my voice cracking. "I'm so sorry."

Adrian reassured me nothing was my fault as I started crying. I'd disappointed everyone.

We were both quiet for a few seconds. I began to think that he was leaving for Korea in a few days, and I didn't want him to leave with our lives up in shambles as it was.

"It'll be OK," he reassured me.

I wanted to believe him, but somehow, when he said it this time, I knew it wouldn't be okay for a long time.

Chapter 4

Nature's Course

A few days after Adrian left for Korea I fell into a depression. I missed him immediately. I felt alone in this whole situation.

I was heartbroken, playing all the sad love songs I downloaded off LimeWire (a music platform where you can download illegal copyrighted music for free). I had curated a love song playlist and burnt them to CDs that I played over and over every day. During and after school, I spent time writing him letters professing my love and how I longed to see him. He was part of my healing process. Adrian called me on my cell phone after 9 p.m., my time, when my minutes were free. Back then we didn't have the luxury of talking on our cell phones at any time we wanted. Cell phone plans usually came with a certain number of minutes you could use during the day and could talk freely at night from the hours of 9 p.m. to 6 a.m. But the worst part about it was the time zone difference. His mornings were my nights, and I was usually competing with his daily duties during deployment.

My mom was still giving me the silent treatment. Everything she said was to the point and cold. I could still hear the disappointment in her voice when she spoke to me. But oddly, she was still taking care of me. She's such a huge nurturer she couldn't not take care of me.

She'd made a doctor's appointment for me with her OB/GYN to make her feel more comfortable and so that he could have access to the medical information. My headaches and cramping were becoming more frequent, and I knew nature was taking its course. My body was going through changes I'd never known could happen and it was terrifying. At the doctor's office I took another blood test which showed declining HCG levels. They did an ultrasound and there was a very small dot on the screen, but no heartbeat was detected. It was confirmed I had miscarried. Gratefully, I was not too far along in the pregnancy, and the doctor confirmed that the fetus would most likely pass naturally, and I wouldn't need surgery. The doctor prescribed some medication to help aid the process. The doctor also told my mom that I'd need quite a few pads, plenty of rest, and that I'd have heavy bleeding and cramps for several days as everything passed.

I was distraught and disappointed. I was going to give Adrian his first child and now my body had failed me. After sitting with the thought of having a child I'd come to want to have the baby. I wanted to start a family with him. I wanted to get married. I think it was Adrian being away that caused this change of heart about the pregnancy. Yet, I thought I should be happy. I was given a second chance at not being a teen mother. But that wasn't enough to ease the grieving of the miscarriage.

I remember crying so much during that time. I cried in the doctor's office. Then I went home and cried in my room. I cried telling Adrian on the phone. I just cried, cried, cried. I didn't feel like I had any support. Momma sure wasn't going to hold my hand and hug me about it. I felt so alone. I felt empty as I prepared for nature to take its course.

The bleeding started like a heavy period, but I knew it wasn't. Every trip to the restroom was overwhelmingly emotional. I started to block it out and just go through it. Even though Momma was still upset with me she did check on me to make sure I was okay. The entire process went on for about a week and a half. I bled heavily and cramped most of the time, going back and forth between curled up in my bed and sitting on the toilet in the bathroom trying to find some relief from the pain. The house was quiet like the peace had been disrupted, but I grew up where we didn't really discuss the trauma. We just went through it. It was all unbearable. I knew my sisters had pieced it all together and they looked at me with pity and offered to do small chores for me. Adrian expressed how he felt helpless through it all. We emailed and called often, but I told him I was doing fine to ease his helplessness because honestly it was nothing he could do all the way in Korea. I spared him the graphic details of what I was going through in my body. I felt guilty enough and I didn't need him to feel sorry for me. Although he was very sympathetic and apologetic, he couldn't be there for me.

    All I was thinking about was that I couldn't wait for life to get back to normal. I wanted my body back. I wanted Momma back. I wanted peace back. I wanted to start fresh, honestly. I no longer wanted this hanging over my head every second of the day. The one time I tried to apologize and tell Momma how sorry I was and that I made a mistake she cut me off and struggled to contain her feelings before walking away.

    I cried to Adrian one night when he called, breaking down, and explaining that I wasn't even myself. I was so depressed from everything that had happened since he had left. He told me he'd send me some money so I could get an apartment and leave Momma's house. This had brought me some hope. I remember being giddy hearing him say, "When I come home for mid-tour I'm going to marry you, Fairlen." Adrian could tell me nothing wrong and for the first time in weeks, I smiled.

Chapter 5

The Root

Winter 2001

By winter, I'd finished all my credits to graduate from high school early. I was excited and was looking forward to my future with Adrian. I was in the midst of finalizing an apartment choice for Adrian and me when, out of nowhere, I received a strange message from cousins on my estranged dad's side of the family. The email said my grandmother, Madea, was sick and she wanted to see me because she was terminally ill.

I'd never met my grandmother and had not really had any real interactions with my dad at that point. So, to get word that a grandmother I didn't know wanted to see me was puzzling me. I didn't know anyone on my dad's side of the family. I'd always known who my dad was and knew what he looked like but had not talked to him. The first time that I'd seen him was when I accidentally bumped into him when I was 10 years old and living in my hometown of Pass Christian, Mississippi.

See, I was his secret child, and his wife and family didn't know I existed. I was the first result of Momma's bad dating patterns, which usually included a man with a ring on his finger and a family of his own. These men were inaccessible but financially stable and could provide money when needed. My dad was just the first one.

The day I met my father was an emotional day. It was after a fight and seeing my dad was completely unintentional. It was during the ride home from the church's youth trip. I was sitting with this girl in the van, and I remember her sister was sitting nearby adjacent to us. They were both chubby, high yellow complexioned little girls with a good grade of hair. Honestly, they looked a lot like me. We had very similar features. The subject of our parents came up and one of the girls bragged that her daddy's name was "Bobby."

Bobby? I'd thought to myself as I remember that Momma told me that was my daddy's name. The girl I was sitting with said they lived in De Lisle, which was a town right across from where I lived.

I couldn't resist and naively said, "My daddy's name is Bobby, too and he lives in De Lisle."

That is all I knew about my father, and I was so excited about the commonality I had with these two stranger girls. I was so happy to find that connection. Could they be my sisters? I wanted to know more, but my mom had told me not to say anything to anyone about my dad and I'd already said too much. The expression on the girl's face turned from friendly to outraged. She angrily yelled back at me, "<u>We</u> don't have the same daddy!"

I was immediately taken aback, as my excitement quickly turned into confusion. The two girls began to escalate their voices yelling at me telling me I was wrong about their daddy. I yelled back at them attempting to defend myself.

I didn't understand what they were saying. In my little naïve mind, I wasn't trying to say their daddy was my daddy, but it just seemed to be too coincidental not to be. I just kept thinking, how dare she scream at me like that? The commotion brought on instigating chants of "fight" and "I bet ya' won't hit her" from the other children in the church van and adults stepped in to separate us. I was forced to sit in front of a church van with an adult. I was so mad I started to cry. My young mind was swirling with confusion, curiosity, and shock. My heart was rapidly racing as I kept replaying the argument in my head.

I wasn't trying to be malicious. My dad's name was Bobby and I couldn't understand why they were so upset. Over and over, I was bombarded with an overwhelming sense of misunderstanding. Did my *sister* just try arguing with me? And if so, why? Was she my sister? Was it the same Bobby?

When the Goodwill Missionary Baptist Church van stopped in front of the church, I quietly got out and sat on the steps. I couldn't wait to tell Momma what had happened when I went home that evening. As I was sitting on the steps, still full of confusion, a pea-green station wagon pulled up to the church and idled by the sidewalk. One of the chaperones told the two girls I'd been arguing with to get their things together because they'd be leaving soon, and she'd received word that they'd be going to a funeral.

I remember feeling relieved that I wouldn't have to interact with them for the duration of the rest of the day and they would be gone. As the two girls burst out the church door with their belongings, I put on a mean mug as they ran past me to the station wagon. A tall thin, light complexion man got out and walked around to greet them.

"Daddy!" The girls screamed running to him.

"Hey, babies," he responded, rubbing the top of their heads.

I was in shock. I was stuck.

That was Bobby. My blood ran cold, because the moment I saw his face, I knew for a fact he was my father, Bobby Dedeaux.

He was about 50 feet away standing right there in front of me on the sidewalk. I stared. I couldn't turn away. My heart leaped in excitement. I'd never seen my dad before, and I couldn't take my eyes off of him. I always imagined my dad looked like a Debarge brother and I wasn't too far off. He was 5'9, fair-skinned like me, with a lot of hair and the definition of Creole. I definitely got a few traits from him, no doubts about it.

I was studying him taking a mental picture as his daughters pointed at me and began explaining our fight. It was weird. Like I wanted to run to him and hug him too but knew I couldn't. I was being discussed and it seemed as if time was standing still.

Bobby looked in my direction as the girl said loud enough for me to hear, "And then she said her dad is Bobby and you're her dad!"

He looked at me and I stared back at him.

He saw me. I saw him. We saw each other. I was scared. Up to this point, I only knew of my daddy. I was told never to tell anyone about him and while I didn't understand why, the first time I did, he magically appeared.

"Dad!" The girl said again, interrupting his stare. "She's lying! You aren't her dad."

"Yes. I am." Although he said it loudly it seemed like the world had stopped and it was eerily quiet. His voice was loud and demanding. It floated straight to my ears. He abruptly broke his gaze and turned his attention back to the girls. He opened the door to the station wagon and scooted the girls into the car as they reacted in protest and confusion.

I am! I thought to myself and then stood up.

Now what? I was hoping that he would call out to me so that he could introduce himself properly. I smoothed down my ponytail. I was ready to meet him. I wanted to look presentable, make a good impression on my dad. But he didn't turn in my direction again. Bobby told them to buckle up, slammed their door, trotted around the station wagon and without saying a word to me or looking in my direction again, hopped in the car and drove off.

I stood there, watching as the station wagon turned out of the church parking lot and disappeared down the road. My heart sank and I retreated into the church bathroom where I unleashed a thousand tears. That night I was quiet at dinner and when my mom inquired of my unusual silence, I told it all. I couldn't hold it in another second. I talked a mile a minute, explaining detail by detail of what happened. She looked at me with such concern and quietly listened while eating her food. I was so upset by the whole ordeal.

"Why didn't he say anything to me if he's my dad?" I asked. In that moment, in the only way she could, Momma told it straight and real.

"He's married to those girls' mom," she explained without skipping a beat. I don't think she even put her fork down to have a moment. "He most likely didn't want trouble at home."

That was the full explanation and basically the end of our conversation. 10-year-old me was unable to comprehend it fully, which led me to be even more confused. There was no further explanation of why Momma had a baby by a married man, or why I could never know him. I wanted to know more. But unfortunately, I was raised in a stereotypical Black household. *Don't be asking no questions. Stay out of grown folks' business. Adults only tell you what you need to know, and you accept what they give you.* There were no detailed explanations.

But I had questions; I couldn't help it. Would I ever know my dad? Why didn't he want to know me? Those questions plagued me for years—even haunted me. The questions then turned into wounds that would shape my view on men. I began to believe that I couldn't depend on men, and they'd abandon me easily. I could not trust a man to be there for me when times got real.

And to make matters worse, I'd soon find out that Momma wasn't the only one on his list of women he'd had illegitimate children with and then disappeared in the wind, leaving these women to raise their children alone. The last time we counted there were 21 known children from this rolling stone arrangement. He only raised four of his children that were with his wife.

In those early years, the idea of men was rooted in my young, undeveloped mind. Men gave women money or attention for a short time and had more than one woman and household to take care of. I mean that's what my dad did, and my mom seemed to be alright with it. She never forced him to come to see me or anything. She'd taken care of me and my sisters just fine. My mom handled her business, and she didn't depend on a man to make her life work. She worked extremely hard and made us strong, independent, and hard-working women.

Because of what Momma went through, there was this unconscious conditioning in our minds that we shouldn't expect much from a man and don't depend on men to care for you emotionally or physically in any way. You must have your own and hold your own always. You must be stronger than the cards you are dealt when it comes to men. They cheat. They lie and that's just how men are. Even the nice ones are like that. This is what Momma taught me. Us. I learned to be strong and resilient without a man's presence from Momma. This conditioning kept me with a mindset to always be one step ahead and be prepared for whatever shenanigans men could throw my way. Even though Adrian was solid, I knew not to depend on his every word fully. I knew I needed my own money and a plan b as soon as I could get a job. The generational roots of my learned behavior about men ran deep for several generations.

As young as five years old, I remember my Granny's friend, "Mr. Dewby." He was so nice. He was always giving us candy and he was always at Granny and Grandad's house.

Every Saturday morning, when my Granny would go out to get groceries, Mr. Dewby would pull up in his big Skylark to drive her. I was very confused why Granny was always with this man and not my grandfather. He was almost a permanent fixture around their home often giving my Granny money to support her gambling habit. I'd seen him slip money into her hand many times.

Granny was still very married. My granddad was blind, but he knew about Mr. Dewby because they seemed to be good friends. They'd often sit on the porch, drinking coffee, chopping it up and shooting the breeze about the good ole' days, current events, and barbershop talk. It was not until much later that I was able to understand that Mr. Dewey and my grandmother were having an affair. Due to these interactions very early on, I was subconsciously taught that marriage was not what it was cracked up to be. Marriage was something you could do if you wanted to. I knew it was something I wanted to do. Because of how well Adrian treated me, I somehow made up my mind that he would be the exception. He wasn't perfect, but he was slowing reprograming my mind to trusting men a little. However, as I continued to live and grow in my relationship with Adrian, I would soon discover that I probably should have kept some of my old mindsets about men.

After all that I'd gone through it would take several years and coming into the knowledge of Christ to change my views on men and marriage. It took me witnessing godly examples of healthy marriages to give me hope that there is a possibility of strong relationships. When I saw husbands and wives who actually maintained monogamous relationships and raised families together, I realized that what I had seen as a child was not the "norm," and God's standards were what I wanted to follow to create a marriage that would last. This mature thinking wouldn't come until several years and many hard knocks.

This invitation from my elusive dad's side of the family was surprising, to say the least. I explained to Adrian how random the invitation was and told him I was going to meet Bobby's mom. It was curiosity that was getting to me because of the way Bobby had ignored me at 10 years old; I was shocked his mom even knew I existed. I wanted to know why. After speaking more about it with Adrian, he encouraged me to go and discover my roots, and maybe even learn something about myself.

I couldn't wait to get out of Momma's house. I was tired of trying to fix my big mistake and wanted so badly to escape the tension between her and me. We both needed space so that we could heal, and I thought it would be best for our relationship. So, with that, I decided to go back home to Mississippi.

The secrecy of my existence created this wall that I was finally about to climb over because of the invitation to see my grandmother. Yet this desire for freedom, adventure, and growth was burning in the void of my loss. This trip back home was a break from my reality. I moved away from Pass Christian at 12 years old, and I was excited to see old faces, spaces, and friends when I returned. It felt nostalgic, yet new being back in the streets of Pass Christian. So much had changed and stayed the same in this town of about 5,000 people.

When I finally arrived to meet my other family, it was a breath of fresh air for me. It was such an exciting experience to meet siblings, aunts, uncles, and cousins and see people who literally looked just like me. The few months I spent interacting with various members of my dad's side of the family and Madea was eye-opening. It was both sad and relieving at the same time. When I met Madea, I didn't have long to be with her. Just as soon as I got there to see her my time with her was cut short. Due to her illness, she was quickly put into a medically induced coma. I felt robbed of my time with her.

It hurt me to realize that I'd never get to know Madea the way I'd known my maternal grandmother. I'd never get to experience what she was like and learn things from her. I'd never get to visit her home. I didn't get to know her story. All the memories I had of her are in that nursing home before she passed. When she passed, it was hard for me to feel sad about this stranger. I was more disappointed in the time lost and that I was robbed of an experience with her. Then immediately coming off an emotionally charged time after the miscarriage to the death of a stranger, I was finally introduced to Bobby.

As a child, I always imagined this big ceremony upon meeting him with lots of hugs and confetti, but as I aged, I no longer had a longing for that celebratory connection. I had gotten over it. It was a simple, formal meeting—nothing spectacular because by that time, I had moved on from it. My heart was no longer seeking after him. I was nearly a grown woman who, by now, had had my own life experiences and found my void filler in Adrian.

By the time I met him, I didn't have much to say other than, "Hello." I no longer cared for my questions to be answered. I was empty. I didn't care if he loved me. Or if he wished he had been in my life more. If he was proud of who I'd become. Even to this day, we've never discussed anything about our relationship and we aren't close, but it's understood that whatever wasn't has been put to sleep. I have no desire to resurrect it. He can thank Momma for that. It's how I was raised. She instilled in me to bury any emotions of rejection or abandonment that he may have caused in my heart and move forward. All in all, I never regretted spending those months meeting his side of the family and getting to know everyone. It helped me to understand who I was. A lot of pieces about my childhood began to come together to create a picture that I needed to see a bit more clearly. I had been oblivious to my anonymity as a child.

    I remember in preschool, I had a bus driver who really doted on me. She'd give me candy and snacks and I'd sit right behind her. She really took a liking to me. Come to find out, she was my auntie, one of Bobby's sisters. I met siblings and cousins who I'd seen in school in passing. It was crazy and interesting learning a whole branch of my family tree that never knew I existed had been in my life the entire time. I'd found new pieces of me that explained so much about me like whose smile I had to the back stories of some of my family members and how I have some of their same traits. It was a coming-of-age adventure that I was happy to have gone on the journey.

Somehow, this experience also seemed to bring Adrian and me closer than we'd ever been, although an entire ocean separated us. We missed each other terribly and I couldn't wait for him to come home in July for his mid-tour leave. I quickly returned to Kansas that May, as I had to also get back so that I could graduate with my class and resume my apartment hunting for the two of us.

As soon as I got back to Kansas, Adrian sent me a Western Union transaction for a couple of thousand dollars. I felt extremely grown looking for our first apartment and secured an apartment almost immediately. It was perfect timing as I had recently turned 18 and could sign the lease and move in with no problem. Adrian sent me money regularly for the bills and to slowly furnish the apartment. I felt like a wife preparing her household for her husband as I decorated the apartment and prepared for everything that was about to happen. And when it did, it spun me around so quickly.

I found a simple wedding dress to hang in my closet next to my cap and gown. Despite all I'd faced that year, I proudly walked across the stage as a Class of 2001 graduate, with my mom, aunts, uncles, and sisters cheering me on. My mom and I had slowly gotten to a better place as I called her daily while I was away. We'd always been close in our own way, and it really hurt me to be so emotionally far apart from her.

Adrian was true to his word, and he didn't miss a beat in taking care of me. And honestly, I don't think it was the weight of the unexpected pregnancy. I genuinely feel that he wanted to be there for me and be the man that he was. Everything moved so fast from there. He was home on the first of July. Proposed on the Fourth of July. Then on July 23-my mom's birthday-we got married at the courthouse. In less than 60 days, my whole life had changed. I'd graduated, moved out, and got married.

I would stare at my wedding ring in disbelief at times. It was a beautiful diamond band set. I'd stare at Adrian in disbelief. He was beautiful. Our life was beautiful. I was a wife and in so many ways, I felt I'd beat the odds. So many of the Hall women had never got married. I felt vindicated that despite my earlier turmoil, I'd come out on top. The honeymoon stage was short for Adrian and me as he was only on a mid-tour leave. He returned to Korea shortly after we wed. I took on the supportive military wife role, keeping in touch daily, trying to keep our relationship exciting despite the distance.

It felt so legit at 18 to live a big, grown life. I Skyped with Adrian nightly. Days and nights all started to run together, and I loved my husband but missed him dearly. At times, it felt like a surreal experience being married but always physically alone.

Adrian sent me money regularly to get whatever I wanted. I was great at making our small apartment a home. I was a creative decorator, with a knack for organization and cleaning. I kept the house immaculate. The irony was it didn't feel like a home because it was just me there. I visited my mom and sisters for dinner often but returned to the quiet stillness of our apartment. Although I didn't need money, I stayed busy working and making my own money. Momma always taught me a woman should always be able to provide for herself. And in my alone time I was learning more about myself. In that loneliness, I'd soon come to the realization that I wasn't happy. For the first year of marriage, in my solitude much resentment grew within my heart that would ultimately corrode what we were trying to build. I became confused, and empty and began trying to fill voids that, in retrospect, only God could fill.

    I was loaded down by rejection, isolation, low self-esteem, and other soul issues that were eating at my heart and my marriage. I was trying to stay positive and hold down my home. I don't know if Adrian felt it, but the foundation of our marriage was eroding, and although friendship and love were there, we were on the frontlines in a battle meant to destroy our bond.

Chapter 6

The Distance

Adrian received orders to be stationed at Fort Campbell, Ky., and for the first time in my life, I moved far away from my mom and sisters. This was going to be a big adjustment for me because even in Adrian's absence, during his training and deployments, I had someone to talk to. It was comforting to still be able to visit my mom and sisters or share Sunday dinners at Momma's house and then nap on the couch afterward. I was able to turn to them when I was feeling lonely. It didn't feel like total isolation with my family only a drive away. But I soon found myself preparing to start a new life without them being more than nine hours away.

My heart ached at the thought of leaving my sisters behind. We were the Hall girls, and no one penetrated the bond we had. We had faced everything together, including the huge relocation we went through at a young age.

Momma pulled us up from our roots in Mississippi when I was about to enter middle school and moved us west to

Kansas. When we were in Mississippi, everything was much different. We had our large family, tons of cousins, and extended family and friends to associate with. But when we moved, we found ourselves alone - just the four of us. We had to learn how to depend on each other. Learn to be each other's defense, and our defense was fierce. My sisters and I may have had our differences – who used all of the hot water, whose turn it was to use the phone, who got us in trouble by not doing chores – but we knew when we left the house we were a united front.

We all knew our roles in our sister circle. I was the mom. Since Momma worked a lot, it was often left up to me to make sure my sisters ate dinner, did their homework, and that we were all cleaned up and got in bed on time. Gabby was the protector of the group. She ensured that no one messed with us and if they tried, she ensured there was hell to pay for it. She was also incredibly silly with a big sense of humor. No matter what the mood was, she always had a way of sneaking a joke in to lighten the moment. In a sense, it was one of the ways she protected us. Her humor offered a distraction from our reality and helped us to forget about whatever turmoil we were immediately facing. Monica was the sensitive one. She was the voice of reason, always making sure we thought about the outcome of our decisions. Monica was always neutral and could easily deescalate when Gabby and I had lost our cool.

I loved my sisters dearly, and though I knew I was grown and starting my own life, I felt a bit of guilt like I was leaving my sisters behind. If life were to abandon anyone of us, we as sisters were supposed to be there to pick up the pieces – if I left who would help them? They would be one sister short. I felt they still needed me, and I needed them. It was such a bittersweet time. I knew not having Momma and my sisters around would take me to a new level of homesickness. But nevertheless, I packed up our apartment and the military shipped our belongings to a small home in Clarksville, Tennessee.

Adrian and I had been married for two years and my military wife life wasn't glamorous at all. I knew in high school when he went to Korea how hard it was, but with a full-blown war raging in Iraq I was scared and worried daily as Adrian's orders took him to the other side of the world.

Fort Campbell was a quaint military base, filled with bland brown box buildings and standard military residential housing. The surrounding towns outside the gates, Oak Grove, Kentucky, and Clarksville, Tennessee, held the few things that created some kind of normalcy and entertainment. There was a small mall in Clarksville, and I found a Black hairstylist and nail shop to frequent for my beauty upkeep and maintenance. I quickly acclimated and soon began looking for a job.

I accepted a job at a newly opened call center called Convergys. Convergys had hundreds of workers and provided me with the sense of normalcy and routine I was looking for. It filled a void, and it felt good to start making my own money quickly.

I'd get up early, get dressed for success, and take my place among the dozens of cubicles. I'd spend eight hours taking and making calls. While I didn't really make friends, I would always have funny and meaningful conversations with co-workers.

A group of 20-something-year-olds in nearby cubicles would gather when we were on breaks or in between calls. There was the usual water cooler gossip and silly banter. It was an entertaining camaraderie that made the day go faster and broke up the monotony of the calls.

After work, I'd usually grab a bite and lounge on the couch, watching reality TV for a little while. Then I'd take a hot shower and plop down around 9 p.m. to chat with Adrian. I would be ending my day, and he'd be starting his in Iraq where it was about 6 a.m.

I also found a church to worship at called Faith Mission Ministries. A co-worker had invited me to her church, and I began going sporadically. It wasn't regular, but when I felt moved to attend I'd pop in for a little worship.

In June 2003, déjà vu struck, but this time, joy abounded. Adrian had recently come home on a mid-tour leave, and we enjoyed every second together before he left. The next month, I missed my period. My body felt so discombobulated, and I quickly grabbed a drugstore pregnancy test to see if, again, I'd become fruitful. This time, I was alone when I went to the doctor, had testing done, and received confirmation that I was pregnant.

I was excited, scared, and in shock simultaneously and I broke the news to Adrian that night. Hearing his excitement and laughs over the phone made me smile. I was happy too, because this felt like a second chance, and it was free from any dread or guilt. We were building our family.

I was excited to tell Momma this time, and I knew she'd be genuinely happy to have her first grandchild. It brought so much joy to my heart to hear her clapping and squealing with glee as I told her on the phone. This helped us further the healing between us, and it was therapeutic for me. She cried with excitement, and even before my baby was born, she proudly proclaimed that my bundle of joy would be *Mimi's baby*.

As my pregnancy progressed, a fear lived in the back of my brain that history would repeat itself and I'd lose my child due to a miscarriage. But with every appointment, strong heartbeats would increase my confidence. I studied every flutter. I cherished every kick month after month as my stomach grew into a round bump. I fell in love with my baby, and my fears dissipated. Eventually we found out we were having a boy and decided to name him AJ.

Witnessing creation within me somehow opened a portal in my soul, and it began to draw me closer to God. I was praying so much to God about my unborn child and for his protection while he was in the womb and for when he would be out of the womb. I felt so honored and chosen to do this work of growing a life within me. I began to understand that my relationship with God would determine AJ's and I wanted our family to be blessed. Praying for AJ soon became a ritual for me, and even to this day, I have never stopped praying for him.

Becoming a mom felt surreal but also familiar. As the oldest girl, I was used to helping raise children and had a natural leadership/mom-like quality. I was grateful that Adrian was eventually able to be home with me during most of my pregnancy.

It was such a sweet time and one of the happier times that I would never forget. I still smile as I recall how Adrian would talk to my stomach and gazed at ultrasounds. We did so much planning together while he was home. He was so in love with me and the baby and didn't want to leave our sides.

But of course, the military didn't allow our happy times to last for too long. We soon got the news that Adrian was going to be deployed again. I was devastated as I would be nine months pregnant when he did. By this time, I was beginning to pack on emotional baggage along with the pregnancy weight. Insecurity began to build up in me as I realized I was going to be alone, yet again. Young and married with an absent husband, bringing a son into the world to raise him that first year by myself.

In my final weeks, I decided I couldn't stay in this military town to have my baby alone. I quickly took maternity leave and flew home to Kansas to be closer to my family. I couldn't risk my mental health and being all alone in a town where I had no support and to fend for myself as my husband was across the world.

When AJ was born on March 26, 2003, Adrian was still deployed in Iraq. He couldn't come home to be by my side, although I knew he wanted to. Although I knew it was impossible it didn't stop me from hoping for a miracle to happen and that Adrian would come rushing into the delivery room at the nick of time to see his son being born. But unfortunately, that miracle didn't happen that day, it was just me and Momma in the delivery room.

And to make matters worse, my birth had to be induced because I was preeclamptic. Momma was relieved I was home because it gave her the opportunity to be there for me – I couldn't imagine going through that all by myself. And even as a military wife, there were no special treatments for me. It wasn't the experience I was hoping for, but I got through it. Momma was happy to fill in. Her joy filled the whole hospital with sunshine. She was so infatuated with AJ. She didn't want to put him down. She constantly rocked him, fed him, and talked to him as I rested. She proudly took him as *her baby*, and it was that strength for me that helped me make it through.

Another part of my heart healed watching Momma bond with AJ.

But for Adrian and me it was bittersweet. It sadden me that the first time Adrian would see his son was through a video call. I could see the disappointment and joy all over Adrian's face. He was hurt, but at the same time happy to have a healthy baby boy.

I made sure to soak up all the fun time with Momma, Gabby, and Monica, who were still in high school and were so excited to fulfill their aunty duties. I got to enjoy Momma's delicious home-cooked meals and embraced the laughter we shared in the house. At times it was tearful joy seeing AJ be spoiled by his Mimi and aunties. I laughed hearing them baby-talk to AJ and remember thinking it was what I'd imagined the dynamic would be between my child and family. Every chance they got Momma and my sisters were sure to steal as many *suggas* as they could because they knew I'd be leaving soon.

I stayed with Momma for about six weeks before returning to the military base with AJ. I'm not a huge crier but leaving Kansas at that time was very emotional for me. I'd become comfortable with my family's support and missed the feeling of familiarity.

I drove back to Tennessee alone with AJ. Throughout the drive, I was going through bouts of sadness about having to leave my family. I was thankful that AJ slept the majority of the nine-hour trip, as I'm not sure how I would have handled my melancholy mood and his crying the entire ride.

Being back in Fort Campbell alone with a newborn was harder than I thought, but I needed to return to work. But immediately, I could understand all that Momma was attempting to shield me from when I had gotten pregnant as a teenager. Although I was married, I was still alone. Everything Momma warned me about single parenthood began to surface right before my eyes.

I had begun to grow frustrated trying to do it all on my own. I was getting very little sleep and tired was an understatement. There was no break and no help. When my baby cried or needed anything I had to snap out of it and get it done. I was on an invisible hamster wheel and on autopilot most of the day. Leaving AJ to go back to work was so heart-wrenching. But I had no other choice but to put him in daycare as I went back to work. I was hoping that returning to my life of routine would help shake some of the depression that was trying to set in. There was a great heaviness that constantly burdened me. I was doing my best to move past it, but it was not easy.

Everything was on my shoulders as I tried to be a super mom. While I cherished every moment with my baby boy, I also cried every day. Often, I'd be praying and weeping in the shower letting the droplets rinse away my sorrow and stepping out to face another busy day. I couldn't explain why it was so difficult for me to shake my negative thinking. The crying spells were coming more often, and then I soon realized I was suffering from postpartum depression. I really tried hard to fight through it, but eventually, it got the best of me. And I shouldn't have been surprised by it. I was living in the perfect cocktail of life that created the space for me to be enveloped by this crimpling depression.

AJ was about five months old when the military sent Adrian home. I eventually reached out for support through the military health resources, and they allowed Adrian to come home to help me. I was in complete collapse, and I'm not sure I would have recovered if they hadn't allowed Adrian to be there with me.

The respite was nice while it lasted. For a short while, I was happy to finally have my family together. It was such a beautiful time, and it felt new as we experienced parenthood together. Adrian was a great, attentive father. Watching Adrian hold and bond with AJ was refreshing and reignited that endearment I had for him as a caring person who wanted to take care of us. It felt natural.

Giving AJ baths together, laughing at diaper blowouts, and engaging in all the baby talk and cuddles together solidified us as parents. For the first time, we felt like a team. It was a family dream, but it was short-lived. Just like that, Adrian went back to Iraq after a couple of weeks.

Over the course of our marriage, those happy family moments kept me appeased. However, the moments became fewer and harder to hold on to as my solitary life began to wear me down. Life became a blur as I mothered and worked. I was "holding it down" and surviving with a young child.

Adrian and I weren't on bad terms. We just lived in two different worlds and led two different lives. The disconnect caused me to start emotionally distancing myself as unhappiness and loneliness consumed me.

When he did have his mid-tour leaves to come home, it was like having a stranger in the house at times. It'd be the small things that made me realize how unorthodox our marriage was. For example, he never knew where anything in the house was, and he needed directions to go anywhere in town.

Adrian was changing too, and rightly so. He was facing life-altering situations while deployed and would have to assimilate to civilian life when he was home. His driving was even different, faster, and I'd often joke and remind him that he had to follow the rules of the road for the United States.

In retrospect, I realize as our situation progressed, I thought I was being a good military wife, but I really didn't know how to be a wife. I had no textbook example to model behavior after. Nobody had shown me what it meant to be a wife. There were no classes I could take to give me pointers. When I was in the church, they said things like, *be submissive* and *cleave to your spouse*, but I'd never seen it in action even to understand what that truly meant.

I was truly winging the whole idea of marriage and being a wife. I honestly thought I was doing the best for my family, but I couldn't help oftentimes feeling like I was the one being left out. Some may have thought I didn't appreciate a man who wanted a stable family, but I couldn't shake the feeling that no one cared about how I was feeling.

We both continued to do the best we could. But the truth was Adrian didn't know how to be a husband either. Sure, he supported me by providing for us and sending Western Union transfers as often as he could. But the distant "I love you" and "I miss you" would only go so far – I needed more. I'm not sure that there would have been anything he could have done to prepare me for this empty life as a military spouse. Eventually, after months and months, the distance began to wear on our family, and our relationship began to suffer.

As AJ grew into toddlerhood, his conversations with his dad tore me apart. He didn't understand why his dad wasn't there. He had missed so many milestones, including AJ's crawling, first steps, first words, and first birthday. AJ was saying, "Dada," but Dada wasn't there to hear it.

Destruction felt imminent, but I wanted our marriage to work. It felt like being in a war with no weapons and hand-to-hand combat would only get us so far until it was all over.

It was all a big blur of life, a season of confusion and growth as a mother and woman. Adrian was a very quiet person, and he hated confrontation. My personality turned my resentment of his absence into demands. To pacify me he gave me whatever I wanted without question. A new car, money, and even money for surgery. He just wanted to see me happy, but no matter how much I tried, and unfortunately, no matter how hard he tried – and he tried hard - nothing worked.

Adrian would often ask me if everything was okay. I'd say it was, but I knew I was not okay with this definition of love, marriage, and family.

Chapter 7

Big Girl No More

After I had AJ, my weight increased greatly. I'd always been plus-sized, but with the baby weight hanging around, I was getting depressed by my self-image.

I didn't think I had low self-esteem because I knew I was an attractive woman. I took pride in my appearance, always trying to be well put together and keep a professional style. I kept my hair and nails done, and I looked nice and presentable, but I didn't feel good about myself when I looked in the mirror. I was at the heaviest weight I'd ever been. And often wished I'd appreciated my old weight before the baby, but now I was really a *big girl*. The scale tipped over 300 pounds, and after much thought and prayer, and failed attempts at losing weight, I decided to try weight loss surgery.

It was nerve-racking and emotional undergoing gastric bypass surgery. Adrian had supported my decision by telling me he loved me as I was but encouraged me to do whatever made me happy and reassuring me that he would have my back.

I believed being skinny, fitting into cute clothes, and not having to prove I was confident or that I was "pretty for a big girl" would give me the boost I needed to reach true happiness. I'd had a *big girl complex* my entire life. I'd been a chubby kid and a curvy teen. Too many times, I'd be told that I was attractive, but whenever they added - for a big girl - after every compliment it stung deep.

I was a baddie, period. And while I'd convinced myself of it, I believed that if I lost weight, I'd feel and look the way I wanted to be seen by everyone else. I'd also be a good example to my child. I was still young and, unfortunately, still cared about how others saw me. It's funny how everyone seemed to automatically question my confidence in myself. Also, some would rudely, although they thought they were being helpful, tell me they believed I could go further in life, in my career, and it would increase the quality of my life if I were to continue to lose weight. This was something I dreamt about for a long time.

I knew it'd make my life easier all around. I wanted to be healthy and live a long life for my child. I'd convinced myself that the weight loss was primarily for health reasons—avoiding some predisposed issues such as high blood pressure and diabetes and taking control of my future. Shoot, just walking upstairs and getting in a car would be easier. But there was also some vanity mixed in with my reasons for getting the surgery.

The laparoscopic weight loss surgery was successful, and even as I healed, I felt equipped with the tools to reach my goal. I was motivated, and soon, I found myself in the gym working out and eating healthier.

After surgery, the weight continued to fall off. I was so excited every time I stepped on the scale. It became a welcoming friend as I dropped ten pounds or more weekly. My clothes quickly became loose, and I was rapidly approaching my goal of 150 pounds half my size.

The more I lost, the more I noticed more eyes on me. And not just any eyes, the eyes of attractive Black men. My smile and walk became more confident, and I had more energy and less stress on my body.

I'd never been concerned about getting attention, but when you're a big girl you become invisible at times. You are counted out and face so many stigmas. It isn't easy, and I'd become accustomed to holding my head high and just being the best me despite what anyone thought or what the numbers on the scale said.

With the weight loss, I was not invisible, and I must admit I enjoyed receiving the attention. This new me was ready to start new. I was always happy to talk to Adrian, but it seemed to be more about business than it was about our relationship. I'd unconsciously started giving up on my marriage and emotionally distancing myself. I remained cordial and light, but my mind began to wander elsewhere.

Adrian was still my friend above all else. He continued to celebrate my wins with me. But I'd begun to think of him as out of sight and out of mind. I felt free and like there was more for me in this new life I was beginning to live. While I wouldn't admit it aloud, I felt there was still room for me to find real love and the relationship I deserved where I wasn't alone.

Chapter 8

Attention

Summer/Fall 2005

I met Lionel when I first moved to Clarksville and was working at the Convergys Call Center. When I started working there, I had not had my weight loss surgery yet, and he, like many, didn't initially recognize me until we later crossed paths in the future.

If you asked me then if this random co-worker would completely change the trajectory of my life, I would have emphatically told anyone no. But life's paths are funny. They cross, intersect, and loop back in such strange ways. The path between casually knowing Lionel and becoming reacquainted with him was littered with self-realizations about my low self-image, a marriage growing more strained by the day, a total physical transformation of my body, and an influence that made those details in my life collide in a destructive way.

Lionel always came to work in a suit and tie and carried a briefcase. It was a bit of overkill for the job that paid $13 per hour, but it was also impressive. What guy in his early 20s dressed like that? It was somewhat a breath of fresh air from the many baggy-clothed men I was used to seeing. He seemed to be business minded and I noted that. But it was a fleeting thought. I was married with a child, and I loved Adrian even if we were in a long-distance and strained marriage. Lionel and I worked the same shift and sat a few cubicles from each other. A group of about five of us would laugh, joke, and bring light moments to the long workdays, and Lionel was often a part of that group.

When we first met, I saw him as everyone else saw him. He was a cool, funny, charismatic, handsome, well-dressed man. He always smelled good and had a swag that lingered whenever he was in the room. Yet he was kind of, well, geeky. He was thin, tall, and wore glasses.

It wasn't a crime that I'd noticed that he was handsome and funny. He was the comic relief and a bit of eye candy I needed to break up the monotony of the day.

The intersection of this life path connected when a horrific storm called Hurricane Katrina hit land. The symbolic storm in my life followed swiftly. Katrina beat, ravaged, drowned, strangled, and wrapped her destructive arms around the city of New Orleans and squeezed the life out of it. August 23-31, 2005 was a week of devastating destruction and left thousands dead and even more homeless.

One of the thousands left with nothing but memories under murky waters was my cousin, Dee Dee. She blew into my life with love, but her presence was quite tumultuous and devastating in retrospect. I wanted the excitement of the thunder and lightning that came with Dee Dee. Frankly, she was fun and created a socialite lifestyle for us.

Dee Dee came to stay with me in Clarksville for about a month or so to get on her feet. I was alone in the home at the time because Momma had taken AJ, who was 3 years old at the time, for a couple of months so I could heal from surgery and focus on my life without too much stress. AJ would be with her for a couple of months as I reset my life and took some time for myself. Momma was a lifesaver.

I was appreciative of her for that time to focus on my mental and physical health and knew AJ would love to bond with his Mimi. I missed him, and the house was so quiet. I had settled into a boring routine of working, going to the gym, and talking to Adrian trying to still piece together and fix what was just a shell of us.

But with Dee Dee around, she was good company and a fun roommate. We were both looking for a new beginning. Dee Dee was starting her life over and building from nothing. She was content searching for temporary highs and feelings of control because nothing in her life was in her control. She was displaced and chasing highs to forget about all that had disrupted everything she knew.

The weight just continued to melt off me. With every pound I shed, I took a step further out of my depression. I sweated out the loneliness of single motherhood, army wife life, and consumed self-assurance and self-worth. The new Fairlen wasn't afraid to be seen. By the time Dee Dee saw me, she almost didn't recognize me.

"Look at 'cha, Meh Baybeee!" she said in the only way NOLA folks spoke.

Dee Dee was funny and exciting. She loved a little drama and a lot of adventure. She loved to dance and party, which I believe filled a void of loneliness in her life. I quickly welcomed her vibrancy into my life as she brought freshness to my boring routine lifestyle.

Almost as soon as she arrived, she wanted to go to the local club to shake it up. She said she missed it, and in NOLA, it was epic, but she knew it'd never be the same. She was grieving her city and the loss of her lifestyle. I felt making her feel at home and comfortable was the best way to comfort her. In a way, I was grieving, too. It was the loss of my marriage and the inability to fix it.

Dee Dee and I went shopping since I had no clubbing clothes. I was shocked that I could fit in a size I'd never been able to before. I was in the single digits and couldn't believe it. Dee Dee convinced me to buy this short dress and high heels. I'd never felt comfortable dressing like that, but I did look good.

When you are bigger, you have to worry about *this* being tucked, *that* sweating, *this* being smoothed, and none of *it* showing through your Spanx. I was almost at my goal weight, and I could do one of those fat pants commercials where they hid behind the big pants and then dropped them with the thumbs up.

Never being one to show off or brag, I was really feeling the new Fairlen for the first time and found myself looking in the mirror more. I looked cute.

Dee Dee was very attractive and carried herself with a lot of style and pizzazz. She demanded the room and attention wherever she went and could say the right words to get a man to smile and melt in her hands. I laughed watching her work her magic. I picked up all the tips along the way and soon could do it better than her. We laughed like teenage girls as we partied and lived it up each weekend. While married, I felt this was what I was supposed to do in my 20s, right!? We soon had a weekend routine frequenting several local clubs and bars.

She would tell me "watch this" and somehow in five minutes we'd be at a bar ordering drinks, laughing it up, with a group of fine men in our presence. There was a lot of attention on me and for the first time I was okay with it.

The void I had was filled with random men complimenting me, dancing with me, buying me drinks, and using their best lines to get my number. It was like a game. I became an avid player. Then I'd go home and be mom and wife on the phone. It became my new norm. Work hard all week and then dance, drink, and sweat away the stress with Dee Dee. This was way before the days of posting everything on social media, so it was easy to live it up and have no evidence to show.

Dee Dee often got us into interesting situations. Once, a celebrity flew us out for the weekend. That was a weekend I'll never forget, and it showed me that this game of attention I was playing was becoming more than a game and more of an avenue for bad decision-making. The drinking and flirting had led to more physical encounters.

The heart is funny, though, and I was convinced it was all in good fun. I regretted it on the plane ride home, but I also knew I could leave it whenever and just work on being a better me. Besides, I was not getting anything from my husband and

I had needs, so it was understandable even if it wasn't right, right?

It was a typical night out for Dee Dee and me in Summer of 2005. The air was hot and dank, and we were rolling with the windows down, the wind blowing and our music loud.

Lipstick glided, perfume sprayed, and soon we were pulling up to the local Kickers club in our *freakum dresses*. We had planned to kick it hard – and we did not disappoint. We parked, turned the music and air conditioning up and danced, primped, and took a few shots to pregame. Dee Dee talked the bouncer into letting us in for free and then the real question was - who was buying us drinks tonight?

Kickers was always packed with 20-somethings and college kids. It was a typical club that smelled of alcohol and sweat, but the music and drinks were good. The dance floor fog was thick and smelled like old syrup. It was always a packed place, always super loud. The cramped place always led to unwanted hands on your back or butt as you squeezed through the crowd and tried to find a spot to breathe, talk, drink, and two-step.

Dee Dee spoke to this side of me that had always been more reserved, loyal, quiet, and chill. Somewhere between a Long Island Iced Tea and a line dance, I was whisked into a mixed crowd next to Dee Dee, who was with a group of men and that is the moment I encountered Lionel for the first time after leaving Convergys.

It wasn't a magical moment or anything like that. It was super chill and friendly. I noticed how he was dressed and that he was wearing glasses. He was tall, thin, and had this certain swag. Neither of us recognized each other from our previous time as colleagues.

Lionel kept looking at me. Not flirty, but almost confused. It was that look someone gives you when they think you aren't looking, and they are trying to figure something out. Through his glasses, he was still squinting in my direction in this dim-lit club. It was annoying and hilarious at the same time. I felt his gaze burning in the side of my face. At first, I ignored his gaze then stared back at him. He smiled and came over to speak.

"You look familiar, ma," he said.

"Really!?" I replied. "Well, I don't think I know you."

"No. I will never forget a face. You from here?" he asked, then asked me a bunch of local questions.

Then the light bulb went off for him. He snapped his fingers.

"Did you work at Convergys?" He asked.

I had. I then started giving him the same look he was giving me. He seemed pretty familiar, too. Light bulb. He was that guy who dressed up all the time with the briefcase. He was cute, yeah.

We both started laughing as we vaguely remembered each other. We reintroduced ourselves by name, yelling over the loud music.

"You look really different," Lionel yelled.

"I know. I look good," I retorted playfully, flipping my hair.

"OK. Ms. Confident. I see you. Yes, you do!" He said loudly, chuckling.

He was handsome, caramel brown-skinned, and hung his suits on a slim frame. He smelled great and I quickly ascertained that he could talk to anyone.

In those few minutes standing there in the club talking to him, so many people came up and talked to him, gave him a dap, a handshake, and just acknowledged his presence. He always had the perfect response that made the other person smile. He was Mr. Popular and people were drawn to him. I was drawn to him and the way he looked at me I could tell the feeling was mutual.

He bought me a drink and soon we were again yelling in each other's ears over the loud music, our faces close and warm energy passing between us. I could smell the Hennessey on his breath mingled with his cologne. He pulled out his Blackberry, handed me his phone and told me to put my number in his phone. He took my phone and did the same. We parted with a mutual feeling of friendly intrigue.

But the intrigue didn't last as by morning, my hang over had caused me to forget about him.

Chapter 9

Brewing

The way my mind was set up, I was still married and not trying to get caught up in any public foolery. Flirting was cool, and I'd accept a drink or two, but when I got home, none of that came with me.

As odd as it may sound, I didn't really think it was a huge deal to give out my number or even go on a date here and there. Of course, I didn't want to hurt my husband, but I also wanted to live my life and not be permanently waiting until he came home for love and affection. Besides, men did it all the time – which was the story I told myself to justify my actions. I was never committed to any of these one-night, drink-buying, flirting club dudes anyway.

Besides, it wasn't taboo in my family. It was the norm. Grandma had a Mr. Dewby, and Momma always had Bobby or whoever to entertain her. Having a little Lionel to talk to wasn't a big deal. I was still a good woman, a hard worker, and a good wife.

That's what I'd convinced myself.

Playing this little game was irresponsible and self-destructive, and I'd thought I had control over it —until Lionel proved me a liar. Lionel's number sat in my phone collecting digital dust for weeks. A whole month passed. He wasn't on my radar at all. Then, one day, I got a random text message from him asking if I'd forgotten him.

Umm... actually, I had begun to type and then inserted an oops face emoji. I quickly deleted it and simply responded, *What's up!*

Lionel didn't respond immediately to my text, but he did call me later that day. I didn't pick up, and he left a message. I didn't return the call. He called a few days later, and again, I conveniently *missed* the call. I wasn't playing hard to get, I was just busy and did not want to be bothered.

Finally, after calling and leaving messages several times with me not replying, he left a message saying that he was tired of chasing me. He sounded irritated and kind of told me off, calling me rude in so many words. I thought about it and decided I'd give him one phone call. The way he told me off so bluntly, made me kind of smile. He was so blunt. *How dare he, but okay,* I thought to myself.

The first time we talked, it was very natural. He joked about chasing me for weeks, and his tone was different from the voicemail he'd left. He was super easy to talk to, and I found myself laughing at him and really engaged in the conversation. The more we talked, the more it brought back memories of us working at Convergys in the past. I clowned his suits and briefcase, knowing somehow, he'd laugh about it and not take it too seriously.

"What was in that briefcase?" I'd asked him, laughing.

"I'm like Floyd "Money" Mayweather. I carry my millions with me because I don't trust the bank!" He said.

"But you worked at Convergys," I replied quickly and sarcastically laughed.

"That was my job front so the IRS wouldn't come for me," he replied.

I found myself laughing at his ridiculousness and remembering how much he cut up when we worked at

Convergys. I'd sat a few cubicles down from Lionel and always had a convenient front seat to Lionel's behavior.

He'd paid no attention to me at that time. I was the cool, big girl. We'd speak in passing. It was pre-weight loss and while usually I'd brush him off since he couldn't see me then, it was different this time around. Was it fate that he saw me at the club and recognized me? And it didn't feel like he just liked me because I was thinner, but I believed he liked me. It felt like he got me in so many ways. Hours had passed and we were still talking about a little bit of everything. When I got off the phone, I caught myself smiling.

I decided not to talk to him again, but a few days later, he again initiated a conversation. I didn't want to be rude, so I engaged him. Man, he was persistent. The conversation would naturally flow. He was so interested in me. I tried to have short conversations, but he had a way of pulling stories out of me and facts about me - random, silly facts.

We often spent hours texting back and forth:

Lionel: *What's your favorite candy?*

Me: *Laffy Taffy.*

Lionel: *What do you want to do as a career?*

Me: *Something in finance or business.*

Lionel: *Who's your favorite gospel singer?*

Me: *I love Marvin Sapp.*

Lionel: *(Inserts a music note emoji) – Never would have made it.*

Me: *(Inserts laughing emojis imagining his voice as I've heard him sing before) - Awww nah!! I'mma need you to take that down a few notches.*

Lionel: *I don't know what you are talking about, I can sing!*

We discussed the familiarity of growing up in church and religion. This was a subject that was off the table with my husband. In fact, Adrian had refused to go to church with AJ and me. It was so important to me and he'd shut me down and would never give it a fair chance.

Lionel was a church man. He grew up in the church and worked in churches weekly. Lionel worked at Foster's Funeral Home as funeral director assistant to his father, Lionel Montgomery, Sr. He seemed to have had what I considered was a very spiritual side at that time and I could relate to all the things he would talk about when it came to our religious points of views. He talked about the many times he'd faced near-death experiences and that God had to be in his life to keep him mentally. That somehow drew me to him and caused me to sympathize with him. Having someone to talk about God with made me want to talk to him more, ironically.

Foster's Funeral Home was a historic Black funeral home and a pillar in the Black community there in Clarksville. The Montgomery family name carried weight in the community. There was prestige and upper class attached to their name. Their ties in the community connected them to church officials, politicians, businessmen, and more. The legacy he carried as Lionel Montgomery Sr's son was extremely important to him, and he later admitted he often struggled to live up to the pressure of making the family proud.

Lionel knew he would inherit a big business, that for decades, had served the Black community of Clarksville and took care of generations of families at their most vulnerable time. Foster's had laid thousands of people to rest, in a dignified manner. Even if in life people weren't respected for their race, in death Foster's made sure they had all the pomp and life celebration their family wanted. Death is a business and they were good at it. I was intrigued and morbidly interested in all that Lionel did daily working at the funeral home.

Lionel was asking me so much about myself and this new Fairlen felt comfortable talking about herself. It felt refreshing that someone wanted to know... me. Lionel was giving me a moment to shine and really be me.

Chemistry was forming faster than I could reel it back. I tried to turn it down and turn it off but found myself reacting, engaging, and very involved in our more frequent conversations. Our conversations began to happen daily. My mind and heart began to have a tug of war.

It was a friendship and there was nothing wrong with being friends, I'd told myself. But my heart kept going and I found myself comparing him to Adrian. While Adrian was a great man, it was little things, simple things that I somehow compounded into big important things.

Lionel makes me laugh. Lionel challenges me. Lionel is spontaneous. Lionel doesn't mind being a bit flashy. Lionel loves God. Lionel is intrigued by me.

Adrian's so stern. Adrian gives me whatever I want. He never pushes back. Adrian is so… army life, all the time. He doesn't talk about God or want to have fun.

I hated to even admit it, but Lionel was filling this void I had. This desire I had, and this need I had to be seen. Not as mom or wife, but just as me, a woman who had changed and grown in so many ways. It wasn't that I wanted to compare, but my conversations with Adrian were more serious, business oriented as of late. His flirting was sarcastic and his life so structured. Lionel was laid-back, cool, funny and we vibed easily. He was fun. After several conversations, Lionel convinced me to let him take me to lunch. Against my better judgment I said yes, and this feeling of secrecy was born.

When Lionel came to pick me up, he opened the car door and there was a huge tube of my favorite candy waiting for me on the seat: Laffy Taffy.

I laughed. It was small, but romantic, and made me feel heard and special. In my early 20s, it was just the game that I needed to keep me interested. The more we talked the more he learned about my life and I realized I wasn't learning much about him. Once I started learning about him, I really started to form a bond and attachment.

"What's important to you?" I'd asked him over our first lunch date.

"Family," he said and explained how he grew up nurtured by his dad and grandma and how one day he wanted his own family.

"Why were you raised by your grandma and dad? What happened to your mom?" I'd asked.

I remember his expression changed and he ordered another drink. "It's a long story," he said, and diverted to talking about the family he wanted.

He painted this perfect picture of his family, a wife, a couple of kids, him running the funeral home and making a lot of money.

"I'm going to need a wife good in finance, business, and real estate," he'd said, looking my way with a flirty face and smiling. "We could take it to another level!"

I'd laughed, as it kind of sounded good. I could picture myself, white gloves directing families into a funeral chapel, dressed in my Sunday's best every day. I could handle the books, the marketing and truly be the first lady and a socialite in the community - Mrs. Lionel Montgomery, Jr. The thought diminished quickly as I remembered I was still married.

As the friendship progressed, I got a glimpse of what life as his woman would feel like. He invited me to his church one Sunday. The thought of a man taking me to church was so inviting. Sitting with him and his family praising felt amazing. It felt like home.

I recall seeing the stares of the certain church goers as I accompanied him to church that Sunday. After the service many came up to meet me and frankly, be nosy. I represented well and his family noticed how I upgraded their son just by how I carried myself.

It was a huge oxymoron for me to be going to church with a man I was on the brink of having an affair with, but God knew I needed to feel a part of something. Church felt good again.

His grandma and dad liked me immediately. She told me to come to the house for dinner after church. Lionel had warned me she could burn in the kitchen and he wasn't lying. She threw down cooking fried chicken, macaroni, sweet potatoes, collard greens, cornbread, and sweet tea. It was a down home, soul food meal, and while I couldn't eat a lot, I enjoyed each bite.

I remember looking around the table at his father, his grandma, him and me. Lionel gave me this huge façade that felt like home. It felt familiar in so many ways: the down-to-earth conversations, the big laughs, the good food, full bellies, the warm fragrant kitchen.

In a town where I literally had no family and my closest family lived hundreds of miles away, being around Lionel and his family felt like a warm hug. I hadn't experienced soul food, family and camaraderie like this in quite some time.

"That was amazing," I told Mrs. Montgomery.

"Thank you!" She responded with a laugh.

"I told ya' grandma don't play in the kitchen," Lionel said, kissing his grandma.

She smiled dotingly at him and told him he'd better be back Saturday for their breakfast date.

After dinner, Lionel and his father soon began talking about business. I was definitely eavesdropping as I helped clear the table. They discussed what funeral services were coming up that week, the deadline for body preparations, what hospitals and homes they needed to pick up bodies from the next day, embalming appointments, obituary printing, and more.

It was probably the first time I saw Lionel incredibly serious, a bit overwhelmed like he was taking in every word and scribbling mental notes that were not fully registering. But Lionel was intrigued by death it seemed. He'd sometimes describe his job with such excitement in his voice. He struggled with the technical side of things.

"Don't you see dead bodies when you close your eyes at night or have nightmares?" I'd asked him one time.

"Yeah, but it's not in a bad way. I don't see the sadness in it. I see the beauty in how we make someone look good for that final farewell. So peaceful, serene, clean… you know? It really is like solving a puzzle sometimes, because we get bodies in all kinds of shapes," he'd explained.

I remember listening to him talk and feeling a bit grossed out and impressed at the same time. It took a strong person to deal with death all day, every day, but he didn't let it steal his joy. He still laughed and was a good person.

I'd begun visiting him at his job. Death was morbid to me, but it was his business and he spoke about it like he worked at Walmart. Whereas my after-work conversations involved customer service and financial transitions, he'd speak about embalming, burials, and family grief.

I got used to it and it wasn't weird after a while. It was just business. Lionel and I had often talked about ways to modernize and help the business excel including an internal makeover and offering more services. I started to daydream about one day owning the funeral home and how we'd run the business. It was something I could see myself helping him with one day. I liked his drive.

Our friendship soon became a relationship, and it wasn't anything I planned. It just happened and we soon had a physical relationship and were a couple sharing a life together.

I found my heart stopping when Adrian would Skype me at night and I'd not answer because Lionel would be lying in my bed.

Everything in my life was starting to collide. The time Momma gave me to get myself together while she took care of my son was coming to an end. Adrian had begun talking to me more about coming home for his mid-tour leave. He was so excited to see AJ and me.

Simultaneously, Lionel and I had become public. It wasn't planned, but it evolved into us being together a lot. His family knew me. His church began to know me. His friends began to know me.

We never discussed it or gave ourselves a title, but soon we were just… together.

One night, as Lionel was lying in my bed, he proposed a question to me.

"When you gone let me marry you?"

I sighed. He knew I was married so I knew what he was asking. He was really asking if I was going to tell Adrian about him and even leave Adrian for him.

That question had been really taunting me for many weeks. The more Lionel showed up and gave me flowers, dates... love. The more I fell for him.

But Adrian was solid. I'd made vows with him. I truly didn't know what I wanted or needed to be happy.

Chapter 10

Marital Affairs

One night on Skype, out of nowhere I uttered a sentence to Adrian that started a conversation I didn't know I was really ready to have. It had been a long silence. The conversation had been awkward and a struggle.

"Adrian, I'm really struggling in this marriage," I said, breaking the silence.

"What do you mean, Fairlen?" He asked cluelessly, but I know he knew it was strained and had changed.

I let it all out in a long monologue about how I needed my husband here and now with me. I was shifting guilt, but it was buying me time to say what I needed to say. I'd never been good at living a double life. It tugged at the genuine person I was at heart. I didn't like keeping secrets and the guilt of Lionel was weighing on me heavily. I rambled on about needing love and affection, about being lonely and temptation taking over.

"Temptation!?" He interrupted.

I continued to explain. I told him I wasn't strong enough to be an army wife and finally I just said it.

"I've been unfaithful to you and you don't deserve it!" Emotion was strong in my voice. A huge lump had formed, and it wasn't going anywhere. The words stung as they came out my mouth, and I know it devastated him.

"What do you mean you've been unfaithful!? When? With who!?" His voice was rising with emotion. I looked at the laptop screen and quickly looked away from his face. "Who is it?!" He demanded, trying to keep his composure.

I took a deep breath and I told him about Lionel. Adrian and I were friends at the root of our relationship and in that sense, it was easy telling him my mistakes, but as my husband, this was the hardest thing I'd ever had to tell him.

I felt horrific telling him over the phone while he was deployed overseas, but I knew it couldn't wait until he came back home or someone messaging him that they'd seen me with another man. The conversation was heart-wrenching.

There was silence and tears on both our parts. Was this really happening? He was my true first love and somehow it all fizzled out and made no sense.

"I want a divorce," I said, through tears.

I felt absolutely horrible and regretted even letting the word divorce slip from my lips, but I couldn't keep living a lie and cheating. He truly didn't deserve that.

All I could do was apologize. Our marriage wasn't bad or riddled with fights or abuse. Our marriage was strained and broken by distance, time, and space. I felt we'd grown apart. I felt he'd been an absent father and husband and maybe we'd be better as co-parents. I felt we both deserved better.

We'd been married five years but only really been together for months at a time as two 18-month deployments had fragmented our time.

The word divorce had left him speechless. He shook his head. He angrily said he couldn't *deal with this right now* and ended the call.

I sat in silence as the call ended not knowing how to feel. I felt free and trapped at the same time. I felt pain and relief. I was no longer living a lie or two separate lives. I felt weird knowing I'd just inadvertently chosen Lionel over my husband and no matter what I did I couldn't take those words back. I'd ruined it.

While I broke up with him my heart was crushed. I felt confused. I wasn't used to him not being a part of my life and he'd went radio silent on me. I emailed him after a week and asked if he was okay. I asked him to call me, just to make sure he was okay. I knew he was under a lot of stress and I could not forgive myself if something bad happened and we never got to speak again.

Eventually he took a call. It was brief. He asked about his son and said he was coming home to see AJ before the end of summer. Lionel noticed my change in demeanor immediately after everything happened with Adrian and me. It was almost like this ego-boosted persona in Lionel had begun to take place. He took pride in knowing *I left my husband for him* and *he'd won the prize* so to speak.

He tried to comfort me in my heartbreak. At the core I felt like I'd been stuck in a tangled web of ignorance and confusion and the more I tried to figure it out the more the web wrapped around me and strangled me.

"I'll take care of you, Fairlen. I promise. I'll take care of you and AJ. You don't have to worry about anything," was Lionel's promise as he held me in his arms, and I grieved the loss of my husband with a deep fear and regret lingering in my heart.

What had I done?

Chapter 11

Broken Triangle

Adrian had contacted me to let me know he was giving me the divorce. I was devastated he agreed to the divorce. Maybe in my head, I pictured him fighting for me and asking me to stay and be a family with our son.

As a young woman, I was so indecisive and went with the flow of whatever happened in my life. Lionel chose me, and Adrian decided he was willing to give up. Adrian made it easy for me, so I decided to stay with Lionel. Deep down, I wanted Adrian to save me from myself. It was wishful thinking to want Adrian, the man who never pushed back with me, who gave me whatever made me happy to stand in the way of something I said would make me happy.

For some reason that infuriated me about him and justified my decision to leave. I couldn't be with anyone who let me go like I was disposable. I know it was my daddy issues rearing its ugly head. The feelings of abandonment and feeling devalued were strong.

With Lionel, at least I went to church and had somewhat of a support system or a sense of family, I'd reassured myself. Quickly, I learned that I'd also signed up for a highly dysfunctional life with Lionel. The persona of this charismatic businessman I'd fallen for soon began to look like a broken, confused little boy with many emotional issues. He came into my life fast, and the tumultuousness of our relationship followed and worsened as time went on. The things I liked about him soon began to collide into huge issues that made me totally resent him.

The relationship was toxic and at the crux of our issues was his irresponsibility with money, his lying, drinking too much, and his emotional issues. This led to a vicious cycle of constant arguments.

I'd caught him in so many lies, things he'd said to make himself sound like something he wasn't. The house he'd said he owned. It was his grandmother's house. Why lie about that?

Lionel couldn't function on his own. He needed me in so many ways. He somehow convinced me to allow him to move in with me and AJ. I soon realized that this was a horrible mistake, as I began to see this man that angered me.

The financial stability he portrayed from the day I met him as he bought rounds of drinks for his friends was all a front and he was incredibly irresponsible with his money. Lionel was often broke. He'd splurge on clothes and alcohol and had an inability to keep proper track of his finances. I'd been raised to take care of my business, pay my bills, and be responsible since I was married and on my own at 18 years old.

As we began to cohabitate, I learned Lionel had no idea of what being a responsible adult meant. We'd decided to split the rent, and often, he'd tell me he'd get me his half in a few days. I was not used to that. My mortgage stayed up-to-date, and my bills were always paid on time. Lionel was borrowing money to pay bills. I was confused. He worked at the funeral home. Where was his money going?

Once, he came home broke and drunk after payday, and I put it all together. Lionel rode the coattails his father had created, and no matter if he had $2 in his pocket or $2,000, he wanted everyone to believe he was *balling*. Instead of giving me money for bills, he'd shoot it away on dice or bets at the club. He was a local socialite and frequented the very place I met him, local clubs and bars fraternizing with his cousins and old schoolmates.

His gambling addiction took him away from home a lot. There was this one gambling spot that he loved to go to. The thing was, he was horrible at gambling, and everyone knew it. They would often take advantage of it, which resulted in him constantly getting scammed out of his money. He was a Montgomery so he was thought of to be *rich* and he had an image to uphold and would never leave the game when he was losing. Instead he'd gamble and drink his entire check away and stumble home to me broken and disheveled.

It was incredibly frustrating that he was not dependable to do his part. He'd always say he'd get the money and he did. His father always bailed him out and took care of his responsibilities. He said his dad said he couldn't have his son begging around town, so he'd front him the money. This dynamic created struggle and anxiety in my life and it was a feeling I did not like at all.

Living with Lionel was like having a disrespectful roommate. I kept my house extremely tidy and clean. Even AJ put his shoes, toys and clothes in its proper place daily or he knew his mom's wrath would be sure to follow. Despite how messy my life may have felt, my home was my haven, and I kept it in order. Growing up in Momma's house, we had cleanliness instilled, beat, and forced upon us, and it had become my OCD habit to have my house spotless.

Lionel had literally created a mess and turmoil in my mind and home. It was trashed, and I wanted him removed. Lionel was a walking oxymoron, he'd have his suits and shirts dry cleaned, just to come home and stuff them in a hamper under dirty clothes.

He was incredibly untidy, and I found myself cleaning up behind him just like I did my four-year-old son. Why was I putting up with this foolery? I don't know. I couldn't even explain it. It was like I wanted to help him overcome his demons. One of his demons came in tall glass bottles of brown liquor and out poured the rest of his legions when he began drinking.

Lionel drank daily, especially after work, that's when it was the heaviest. At first, I thought it was just socially, but then one day I looked in the trash, which he hadn't taken out, and saw so many glass bottles just piled up and it began to bother me.

He drank unchecked on the weekends, binging on alcohol to cope. He drank and drank, spending a ton of money on liquor. He called it "unwinding" and would often sit playing video games with my son and downing cup after cup of Hennessy, whiskey, bourbon- anything brown. It wasn't so much just the alcohol it was who he was when he drank.

A different person appeared when he drank, and it was then that I learned the most about the facade and why he tried to keep it up. As handsome and well-kept as Lionel was on the outside, I only knew a fraction of how distraught and broken he was on the inside.

A few times, while under the influence, he partially told me the story of his mom. The gist was that he'd been told she'd abandoned him when he was a young boy and left him with his father and grandmother. He was torn as he heard various versions of what exactly happened, even the rumor that his father kept her away. He was confused about who to believe but knew his dad had always had his back and would fight for him. Yet, even his grandma, no one, gave him a clear answer and anytime he tried to explain it to me, I was equally confused with answerless questions.

His sorrow and abandonment issues ran deep, and the thought of rejection was a strong theme in his mind. I tried to comfort him and love him through the pain. In retrospect, I even felt somewhat of an emotional attachment to him as I knew the pain of abandonment. Our absent parents weren't dead. They willingly had no connection to us. I empathized with that brokenness at times. Yet, I knew how to keep it together and handle my business despite my broken pieces.

While Lionel talked a big game about us running Foster's Funeral Home one day, he confessed he couldn't pass the state board tests to become a funeral director and mortician. While he knew the business and how to do everything, he struggled with the terms, tests, and technicalities. He'd failed multiple times and lost a lot of money in the process.

Lionel drunkenly confessed to me that he felt like he was constantly losing everything, everyone, and especially himself. I often listened and tried to encourage him, but his brain would be so clouded he'd often spiral. His failures, his pains, and his sorrows all came out as he drowned them, and I tried to be his umbrella and shield him from his dark clouds but to no avail.

I became a casualty in the war Lionel had against himself. He found solace in the socialite Lionel, the baller persona that everyone thought he was. It didn't have to be a weekend, it could be any given night and Lionel would make his way to a place where I guess, *everybody knew his name*.

I realized that everything Lionel said he wanted was him guessing. He didn't want a family or to own a responsible business. He just wanted attention and to be known and seen.

He often did just that, spending multiple weeknights at Kickers buying rounds of drinks, flirting with girls, and showing off. He called it networking and it often kept him out all night.

How dare he allow me to work and he just wasted his life away being irresponsible? He'd come home wasted, disheveled, emotional or sick. It was a recurring nightmare most weeks and we argued a lot over the same things. I'd had to help him to the shower and clean up vomit quite a few times. It was pathetic and the next day I'd tell him he needed therapy and he'd become defensive. We'd begun to argue over all these things that were ruining my peace. I started to regret letting him move in and although he treated AJ well, I didn't like the example he was setting. My agitation was heavy as the months went on.

It'd all reach a roaring climax when the behaviors increased and gone unchanged, and I learned he had been cheating on me. Lionel was cheating on me with his ex-girlfriend, a girl he'd spoken briefly of in the past tense when drunk. She seemed to have broken his heart, but he'd never moved on and had been in contact with her the entire time he was dealing with me.

I first learned about her when my friend saw him and her at a restaurant eating dinner together. He'd lied about his whereabouts. Then a friend of mine texted me a photo of them on a date. When he came home there was hell to pay. It was the worst argument we'd had, and I told him to get out and never return. I later learned he'd run over to her house. He'd been playing us both this entire time. She could have him. I was done.

I deleted his number and started thinking about how my life was at this moment. I'd left my husband. AJ missed his father. I was struggling emotionally and physically, and I was putting up with things I never thought I would.

Lionel had created a cesspool of issues in my life, a conglomeration of confusion, loud chaos, and irritation. Good riddance! I felt total freedom when he moved out and I was putting everything back in order. It was a lesson learned, a moment of realization for me that showed me I could never fix a broken man. I felt it was a clean break and my heart wasn't broken. I felt free.

With Lionel out of the picture, I realized I'd taken for granted all that my marriage had afforded me. Sure, Adrian lacked some qualities I wanted, but he was my stability, my friend, and even in this mess I'd created, he never abandoned the family.

As our divorce proceeded, Adrian and I began to communicate more. He was not even hostile or degrading to me. We still had this mutual chemistry and kindness towards each other. Of course, me cheating was a scathing hot button that neither of us touched. The more he called to talk to AJ, the more the line of communication opened for us to laugh again and smile more with each other.

It was peaceful in the home. Adrian sent money for AJ and me to get back settled. I told him I'd left Lionel and why. I couldn't expect any sympathy and wasn't given any. I reaped what I sowed, right? In a way, it opened the door for us to reconnect. Adrian brought it up as his mid-tour leave approached.

"What do you think about putting the divorce on hold and us trying again?"

I was ecstatic for a second chance. I was starting to see that my life was about continual second chances. I couldn't stop smiling. I knew it took a lot for him to forgive me and move forward, but if he was willing to try, I wanted it just as bad.

It was the first time I saw the clouds start to roll away, and the possibility of having my family back, possibly a rainbow in the distance.

Having Lionel out of my life was like thick smoke clearing. While we were opposite in so many ways, Lionel manifested all my generational curses and exposed and was a reflection of the broken me in so many ways.

Chapter 12

Two Lines

My youngest sister, Monica, and my Aunt Chris had flown in from Kansas to visit me and AJ and to participate in Adrian's welcome home ceremony. It felt good to have family around. For the first time in a long time, I was happy, focused, and ready to move forward in my life.

A couple of days before his homecoming, I'd planned a little dinner for us. Rachael, one of my work buddies, came to my house, and we were going to cook, have a few drinks, and just talk and laugh.

I wanted to drink plenty of big full glasses of wine and celebrate with my family, but this little itchy thought was in the back of my mind. My period had been late. I'd been sexually active with Lionel, but some time had passed. It was likely stress. A fresh pregnancy test was in the back of the drawer in my bathroom. I excused myself and I went to the restroom to take the test.

I don't know why I chose to do it then, but I did. Maybe so I could drink this wine with a free conscience or maybe because I knew my support group was on the other side of the door. Maybe it was because I knew I wasn't, and it'd just be a quick two-minute hiatus from the party. I didn't feel like I did when I was pregnant with AJ, but I was a few days late on my period.

I knew I wasn't. I knew I could put this relationship I'd had with Lionel behind me and move on with my husband with no interference. Pregnancy would just be an incredibly horrific twist of fate and dire consequences for everything I'd gone through. I felt experiencing Lionel had been a lesson learned enough for me. Life could not be that cruel.

I could hear the ladies laughing on the other side of the door as I quietly ripped the test open. I don't know why I was being so quiet, but it was indicative of the secret I'd held.

I peed on the stick, sat it on the counter, and waited. And waited and waited. I quietly sat on the closed toilet trying not to look at the test before my phone's timer went off. When the time was up, I picked up the test and stared at it. Then I looked at the instructions. My blood ran cold. I think my heart stopped for an entire minute as I searched the instructions and reread them over and over.

"If two lines appear, this means you are pregnant," I mumbled, reading the package out loud. The double pink lines looked back at me.

Positive. Positive.

I was reading it right. I almost laughed in disbelief.

Déjà vu. I was 17 all over again.

Two. Pink. Lines.

Two days until Adrian came home.

Two unwanted pregnancies by 24.

Time melted away as I had a total nervous breakdown in my bathroom. I broke down. No. Just. No. This. Was. Not. Happening!

The hopelessness, panic, and total distraught spiraled out of control. I felt like the 17-year-old girl all over again. The shame. The regret. The pain.

How? Why?

The knocks at the bathroom door grew louder.

"Fairlen, you OK! Open up!" Monica said.

I opened the door and my family stared at me. I looked crazy. My face was red, and tear streaked. I was a mess.

They grabbed me to comfort me.

"Baby what's wrong?" Aunt Chris asked with concern, embracing me. I fell into her hug.

"I messed up. I messed up," is all I could get out as I cried.

"Fairlen, it's OK. Tell us what's wrong," Monica said, rubbing my back.

She went quiet and I knew her gaze had found the pregnancy test on the sink counter. I could hear her head whip as she looked back at the test and then at me again. I could hear her and Aunt Chris mouthing the news.

"Girl!" Monica said, sounding confused. She stopped and I could hear her doing the math in her head. She was so thoughtful to not kick me when I was down, but I could tell it all hit her at once.

"It's going to be OK, sis," she said reassuring me. "It's going to be OK."

I shook my head still in utter shock.

I'm pregnant by Lionel. Adrian is coming home in two days.

My life is ruined... again.

Monica is the most sensitive of us sisters and the peacekeeper. She always brings order and peace to calamity in our family. I could read through her emotions and could tell she was freaking out for me despite trying to stay natural and calm.

"Oh, god," she whispered to herself. "It's going to be OK!" She said again.

Monica excused herself to go get me something to drink, but I knew she was taken aback. Aunt Chris talked to me a little, hugged me some more and took me to the living room to sit down.

Rachael was waiting for us and I could tell she'd been ear hustling but was so confused.

"You OK?" Rachel asked.

"Yeah. I'll be ok," I said.

Aunt Chris said it for me, and Rachel tried to hide her reaction.

"Oh wow! Congratulations, Fairlen!" She said uncomfortably.

Aunt Chris shook her head at Rachel, indicating to her that it was not a celebratory occasion.

"Sorry!" Rachel retorted, sipping her wine extra hard.

Everyone was quiet, looking at me with concern.

I hadn't explained the how, but everyone knew Adrian was coming home after a long deployment. I was newly pregnant. I hadn't seen him in months. The math was definitely not mathin'! I was a cheater, and while they were probably shocked and disappointed, they tried to comfort me. I was also relieved that they weren't judging me.

I was so mad at myself. Out of frustration, I blurted out, "I'll just get an abortion."

"Girlfriend, now I don't know about that," Aunt Chris said sternly, looking at me with a look of outrage on her face.

Her solemn expression read, "Have you lost your mind!?"

"Fairlen, you got to give this to God and trust in Him," she said instead.

That quick, I was snapped back into the reality that *we*, our family, never considered abortion as an option. No baby was a mistake, and all babies were Godsent and precious.

"You made your bed, so lay in it!" I could hear Momma say to 17-year-old Fairlen.

They popped a bottle of wine and we had a Waiting-to-Exhale-style girls talk about how I'd got here. Tissues, tears, and a lot of questions later, I felt a cathartic release. I told Rachel, Monica, and Aunt Chris all about my few short months of partying. Then about my whirlwind romance and affair with Lionel, and how Adrian had forgiven me and wanted to reconcile. I made it clear I was ready to be the best mother and wife I could be.

Aunt Chris reassured me it would work out and not to be anxious about what I didn't know. Adrian and I were working on a new us and this was part of me. He could very well accept it.

Monica told me to talk to Adrian and try to work it out. He was a good guy, and we'd been through a lot. She was excited to be an aunt even under these crazy circumstances.

Rachel cheerfully reassured me mixed families work all the time. My family encouraged me and made sure I knew they would be there each step of the way, no matter what. I wanted to believe the positive outlooks, but I also knew Adrian and the news of my pregnancy would not be anything he could forgive.

Chapter 13

The Ultimatum

Two days later Adrian walked into the house after his homecoming and was greeted with applause from us all. We'd cooked like all the other times when we'd celebrate in the past. We had thrown down in the kitchen. Pans upon pans of delicious food lined the counter. AJ ran and jumped into his dad's arms, causing Adrian to drop all his bags.

"Welcome Home!" Monica said, hugging her brother-in-law.

The excitement I'd had at the hanger metamorphosed into pure dread upon realizing I was going to have to tell him. He was home. I had run out of time. I literally wanted to throw up and it wasn't from the baby. I knew I had to ruin our prospect of starting over.

For a few hours, Aunt Chris, Monica and AJ provided family laughter and fun like old times. I was so glad they were there. They shot reassuring looks at me all night and took care of me as they always had. After dinner, my support group gradually left the house, giving me big hugs of encouragement and telling me to call them later. Aunt Chris went with Monica to her hotel to give Adrian and I time.

As the house became empty, I distracted myself by taking over the cleaning from Monica and Aunt Chris. I was wiping the counters over and over practicing the words in my head. I realized there was no good way to say it. Once we were alone, there was no time for talking Adrian quickly whisked me away. It wasn't awkward and like magnets we reconnected easily. We'd always shared a chemistry and passion. It was emotional as we reunited sharing intimacy and passion in our marital bed. All the things we couldn't say, in physical form.

"I missed you," he said, as we lay in bed, quietly.

"I missed you too," I said.

His muscular arms wrapped around my body and stomach and he kissed my cheek. I'd lay still, my eyes looking around searching for the right words. He was genuinely happy. I didn't know if I could do this. How could I just burst his bubble like this? Yet, I couldn't act like nothing was wrong. It was eating me alive and I couldn't even share the bed with him another minute pretending it was perfect. I cringed and moved his hand off my stomach and flipped around to face him.

"I need to tell you something," I said.

It was like déjà vu from the time I told him I was pregnant at 17, except it was totally different. I had to break his heart this time. Adrian tensed up. He could tell by my voice it wasn't good news. When we'd had the talk and I told him I'd ended it with Lionel and was ready to move forward in fixing our marriage, he was genuinely happy and ready to forgive. I just didn't know if he could forgive this but had hoped his love for me was big enough that he could. The look on my face and the quietness that followed was so hard as I searched his face and tried to force the words out my mouth.

The air conditioner kicked on. The smoke detector chirped.

My heart pounded in my ears. My face got hot.

"What's up?" He asked me.

"I'm pregnant," I said, above the thumping of my heart.

Adrian looked at me as if the blood had left his face. His brow deepened into a frown and I could tell he was upset, but he never liked confrontation, so he was trying to keep his cool.

"What?" He said, his voice shaking with emotion. "What do you mean we…"

"*I'm* pregnant," I said slowly, closing my eyes to escape his intense stare.

"It's his isn't it?" He asked in a disgusted tone. He was trying to hold back his burning anger.

"Yeah," I barely said, my eyes fixed on him. I hoped he could see the desperation in my face. "I'm so sorry, Adrian."

He cursed under his breath and quickly got out of bed and stormed out the room. I laid still. I didn't know what to do. Should I follow him? I thought. I just laid there. I started to pray to God to fix it, to fix us, to forgive me, to heal Adrian, to let it work… please!

The fan above our bed whirled slowly.

Full circles.

My life had come full circle from mistakes I repeated.

How could I be so reckless?

I thought about how badly I'd hurt Adrian and totally ruined any reconciliation and how I'd possibly taken AJ's father out of his life with my actions. He'd never forgive me.

I pleaded silently. Adrian, please forgive me.

Adrian loved AJ. He loved children. He loved me. I wasn't going to ask him to stay, but I wanted him to, and I wanted him to accept all of me. The good, the bad, the mistakes. We'd been through so much. We could overcome anything. I knew it. I just hoped he knew it, too.

I prayed hard, my lips moving and tears spilling out. If God could fix this, I promised I'd give this relationship my all and be the best mother to my children. I'd learned my lesson, I promised I'd learned. I just wanted my family back, please. I was at his mercy.

I was at Adrian's mercy.

I prayed so hard I drifted into a light nap and was awakened by the weight of Adrian's body shifting our mattress. I couldn't read him at all. This weird feeling of relief yet heartbreak churned over and over in my head. He had returned. I lay on my side still searching the room and waiting for him to say something. I didn't know if he would say anything.

I was open, raw, vulnerable and in deep pain. Yet, I couldn't imagine his pain and feelings of betrayal. I'd never had a baby with anyone but him. It was a sacred bond. He let out a deep sigh and turned flat on his back, projecting his voice into our room.

"Fairlen, if you want to stay married to me, you need to get an abortion," he said as clear as day.

His words fell on me like acid ripping through my skin. There was more silence. He knew I'd heard him, and he meant it as stern and matter of fact as he said it. Just like that our reconciliation had turned into an all-or-nothing horrific ultimatum.

I did not protest. I was in shock. I lay there, wanting to hug him, wanting to apologize, wanting to figure out another way. I wanted to beg him to accept me and don't ask me to do such an unspeakable thing. In the darkness of our room, a big darkness hung over our bed.

Abortion.

Finality.

Death.

This kind, loving man who I thought would not be fine with it, but at least willing to discuss it had in one sentence determined my future.

Did I want to stay with him?

Did I want this marriage?

I did.

Did I want it more than my child?

"I'll be damned if I raise another man's child," he said, trying to keep his composure and interrupting my thoughts.

How could he ask me to do this when he saw all of what we went through with the miscarriage before AJ? It was backwards the level of betrayal I also felt. I got that he thought I owed him this to mend his heart and restart our future. Without thinking, I simply said, "OK."

I pulled up the covers and silently cried. Tears soaked my pillow, and I freely let them roll. This was a nightmare. How did we get here? The quietness of our marital bed indicated the long-awaited reunion had been completely destroyed.

I felt like he didn't love me at all to ask me to do such a thing. I wanted him to love me enough to raise my child as his own. Maybe it was wishful thinking and maybe I took his unconditional love for granted. But if I was being honest, that's what I wanted him to accept me for all I was, all the mistakes and for the blessing that'd come from the mistake. Maybe I was delusional.

In honesty, I couldn't blame him for his feelings, and had it been me I would've acted a fool and fought him, the baby momma, and anyone else who knew about me and let it happen. I'd never ask him to choose between me and his child though.

Men did this all the time. Men had babies by multiple women, families all over town, just like Bobby and with no consequences. The double-standard of it all was hurtful. I had to choose, and I'd agree to appease his heart. I felt weak and disappointed in myself for the entire situation.

When I woke up the next morning, the regret still weighed on me like a heavy boulder. Adrian's side of the bed was empty, and I realized he was gone. I didn't know what to think. I didn't know where he was or what he was doing. I just knew he was hurt.

I woke up AJ and we turned on early morning cartoons and had chit chat over cereal. He was my son-shine. He could not tell if I was in pain, because that's what's mothers do – hide from their child everything that was going on in my life. I cherished being his mom. I was my best self when I was AJ's mom.

His little footed pajamas swung as he ate his cereal and chatted non-stop. He was so excited and asked me a million questions.

"Where's daddy? Can we go here and there? Where's Aunt Chris? Where's Aunt Mo?"

His little mind was going so fast and his sweet disposition brought joy to me despite the rough night I had. I assured him we would spend lots of time with daddy and have a lot of fun with Aunt Chris and Monica. Soon, Adrian walked through the door. He walked to AJ and kissed him on the top of the head. His smile disappeared as he looked my way.

He put a piece of paper on the counter in front of me. It was a receipt from an advanced checking and loan company for a few hundred dollars that he'd taken out. He'd acted immediately to pay for my abortion.

"Make the appointment," he said firmly, walking out the room.

My heart dropped.

Chapter 14

Aborted

I was in deep turmoil and reluctant, but I made the appointment and a few days later we were on our way to Nashville.

Every second I waited for him to exit the gas station I wanted to somehow escape this situation. I'd always been taught abortion was wrong, and I knew it was wrong, but this was the only way we could work. Adrian was emphatic that this abortion had to happen. It was not negotiable or a conversation. It had to happen if our marriage was going to work. He'd forgiven me for the affair, the fling, but the baby was what broke him.

I went back and forth in my mind on whether I could go through with it. I knew I'd made some bad choices, but I was willing to do what I had to do to make sure my son didn't grow up fatherless like I had.

It was a sacrifice, right? Love was about sacrifice.

I looked towards the gas station window and saw Adrian walking around. His 6'4 frame hovered around the store. My stomach was in knots. This queasiness plagued me, wrapped around my guts, and squeezed me tightly. I felt sick about the whole thing.

I switched the radio to 101.1 the Beat and turned it on low to kill the silence. The beat of the hip-hop music came through the speakers, but my thoughts loudly drowned it out. My mind would not let me rest on going through with this and moving on with my life.

"How could you do this?" My conscience yelled. "How?"

"You're killing your baby!" My conscience confronted me.

"You don't deserve this child anyway!" My conscience teased.

"You deserve this pain!" My conscience punished me.

"You can't do this. You can't do this. You can't do this!" My conscience screamed.

I looked towards the gas station window and saw Adrian approaching the cash register. I felt like a loud clock was ticking. I was running out of time and was at war in my heart. Sweat formed on my brow and my heart started pounding.

"Breath Fairlen," I told myself, but I couldn't catch my breath.

God was watching me. No matter how bad I felt my situation was, I knew God was looking down upon me and I knew I couldn't take away what he was trying to give me. I'd asked him to fix it and I knew abortion wasn't fixing it.

"I don't know who or what this child is or what God has destined for it to do," I thought. "I could be killing a human that holds what the world may need and how could I ever be in the face of God after doing such a thing?"

I closed my eyes and prayed a short prayer, "Help. Me. God." When I opened my eyes, I saw Adrian walking out the store. And in that second, I knew what I had to do. The decision was made. I could not do this. I was not doing this. I'm not killing my child. I'm going to have this baby. I'm not choosing a man over my child. A wave of relief washed over me. In my stubborn determination, that was it. The hard part was letting Adrian go.

I was taught never to let a man see you cry, so I quickly pulled it together, relied on my strength, and put on my straight, poker face.

Adrian got in the car and swung his long legs under the steering wheel. I slowly turned my now red face toward him. He sat his water and peanuts in the middle console and when I looked in his direction, he was looking at me, his brow deep with concern and his eyes pained. It hurt worse. We both knew. We both felt it. We both couldn't live with each other's choices.

"I. Can't." I said, choking back the lump in my throat, but with my most firm resolve. I said it again, louder and bolder. "I'm sorry... I just can't do this. I can't. I won't," I said, turning back in my seat with a finality. "I'm keeping my baby."

Adrian said nothing. He shook his head. Let out a grunt but didn't protest or argue. He sunk into quietness. Again, he always gave me what I wanted like always no matter how he felt. I knew he loved me and we both dug into our boundaries despite that love. He cranked the car up and sped out of the gas station turning the car in the direction to take me home. When we pulled up at the townhouse, I quietly got out of the car and shut the door.

I was exhausted emotionally.

Adrian drove off quickly.

I knew him well enough to know there was nothing I could say to him or do to rectify that moment. It just was what it was. It was the end of our seven-year relationship and our marriage without any further discussion and we both knew it.

Chapter 15

Welcome I'yanna

Summer 2007

I sat on the living room couch, bracing the weight of my round, stretched belly with both my hands. A sharp pain shot through my pelvis, stopping me in my tracks. Wincing quietly in pain, I rubbed my tummy vigorously. Being nine months pregnant, I'd watched my body transform and these last few months had been tough.

"'Yanna, you are acting up," I said to my stomach, breathing, pressing and rubbing the pained area below my swollen, tight abdomen. I could feel the weight of her head resting on my pelvic bone.

I was sweating and out of breath from cleaning the mess left behind from the fight party. I was ready for all these people, most I didn't know, to get out of my townhouse.

The Floyd Mayweather vs. Oscar de la Hoya boxing fight that Cinco de Mayo, brought a house full of family and friends to the townhouse I shared with Lionel. I'd told him I wasn't really up for being around people. I was super pregnant, irritable, big and just wanted to rest, but he insisted.

I knew it was because he'd recently got a big screen TV and wanted to show it off. I mean the fact he'd got mad and broke the last TV was a huge reason for the purchase, but he had to show off this bigger better TV. It's just the kind of thing Lionel did all the time. It's like he needed people to praise his accomplishments, even something as mundane as a TV.

I rolled my eyes in irritation. Despite knowing how he was, I tolerated him, trying to build somewhat of a relationship again with him, trying to create a family. Once I'd decided to keep my baby, Lionel had somehow found his way back into my life and with excitement, at first, wanting to try to be a family. Lionel was excited at the thought of being a father, but I knew, and he showed me throughout my pregnancy that he was not ready, and the pressure was folding him.

Adrian was finalizing our divorce. Truly, I didn't want to be a single mom of two kids. I wasn't happy with my situation, but I put up with it and tried to fix the brokenness.

The house was clearing out at about 11 p.m. and only a few stragglers were hanging out on my couch. Some were inebriated, while others were talking loudly about Mayweather jabbing, punching, and upper cutting his way into infamy. It was a good fight- the few parts I caught.

"You OK?" Shante, Lionel's cousin, asked as she collected red Solo cups from the living room table.

"I think I did too much," I replied. "Probably Braxton Hicks, you know how that goes." I sat still, gripping the broom handle as another sharp pain radiated through my pelvic area.

"Do you want me to call Lionel?" She asked, stopping in her tracks and staring at me.

"No. I'm good," I said, laughing lightly and rocking myself a bit. "I'yanna is just tearing mommy up right now. Probably the spicy chicken I ate."

I had to keep moving to keep my mind off the hormonal rage boiling within me. Choice words were flowing through my head, *"Where the (expletive) is that (expletive)!?"*

"Where is Lionel!?" A lingering guest chimed in simultaneous with my thoughts. "How this dude gone invite me to his party and not be here?" The man said laughing and shaking his head. "I'll get up with y'all," he said as he exited the house.

I wanted to have a fight of my own with Lionel. How was he going to have a whole party and not even be present?

Shante was watching me move but saying nothing. It's that unspoken fear all pregnant women get from onlookers, hoping, praying that the waters don't break, and babies don't decide to enter the world at the most inopportune time.

I went to push a coffee table back in place with my knee and Shante intercepted me. She was nice. I knew she was, in her own way, compensating for her trifling cousin's absence. I was over him.

This was another episode of "The Lionel Show." Each predictable episode started with his excitement about something, then the set-up and my help, and last, he'd go ghost, totally absent. Then cut to the last scene, which always makes me livid, he shows up drunk, smiling… that was his character. He'd start with a "what had happened was…" - a stupid excuse for his behavior. I'd flip out. Cue a laugh track and applause. And scene. I wish I could change the channel.

My life was tuned in to this complicated, frustrating, conundrum called our relationship. It was tumultuous, to say the least. Always emotional and predictably unpredictable when we'd be together or apart. We honestly didn't know ourselves. Each week was different. It was a true, make-up-to-break-up relationship, and it was depressing and exhausting during my pregnancy.

A part of me had just given up on what I wanted in life, because these were the cards I was dealt and I knew I made my bed, so I was ready to pull the covers back and get in it. But this bed was not like any other bed. This bed was more like a hard jail cot, uncomfortable and a consequential confinement of my heart. I stopped in my tracks as another horrific cramp sliced through me. "Ow!" I said laughing in surprise. "This is starting to really hurt."

Shante looked concerned and suggested I take a warm shower to calm the pain.

"Good idea!" I said. "I'm going to lay down afterwards and try to let 'Yanna calm down.

Shante said she'd hang out for a few minutes until Lionel came home so I wouldn't be by myself. I didn't care, but it was nice of her to offer.

"Thank ya, girl," I said politely. Later I was so glad she stayed.

I waddled back to my bedroom and checked my cell phone for the 100th time.

The five text messages I sent were still unanswered.

11:35 p.m.

"*Where the f_u_c...*" I furiously typed on my phone screen and then deleted it in frustration. I wasn't chasing a grown man, but I hated being ignored.

I knew where he most likely were, but a part of me was like, "Naw, he can't be *this* trifling to leave his nine-month pregnant girlfriend at home and go to the club or his little-girlfriend house with a whole party he had planned." But I knew his motives and that's exactly where he was.

He was with her, the ex. I wasn't even jealous. I knew exactly what she had, and I'd bet money he made her the same promises he made me: family life, family business owners, success, love, marriage, all the things he could not truly give anyone because he didn't have it to give. Lionel was playing his role well, but only I saw right through the facade.

He'd invited all those people he knew to watch the big fight, bought all these chicken wings, beers, sandwiches, and basically blew his whole check on this party. I didn't know if he had even accounted for any of the bills.

The way Lionel moved made me want to scream. I was not used to a man who couldn't handle his business and just take care of his family without having to be reminded and begged. Lionel was not dependable and that was the one thing I could depend on.

He'd been at the center of the party for about an hour, drinking, and talking smack super loud with his company, before his Blackberry went off and he'd disappeared upstairs.

I was in the kitchen but could see him clearly in the living room of the townhouse we shared. I watched him move, because I knew since we'd been arguing he'd be up to old antics.

He reappeared with a new outfit on and he and his big cousin had to make a "quick run" to go get ice and some more bottles from the L-store. He and his cousin ran in the same social circles and frequented the same clubs.

I stared at him blankly and said, "Really!? Why can't you send someone else? This is *your* party."

He told me he'd be right back and I knew he was lying. He was good at that. I knew he wasn't coming back. I saw right through him as he checked his Blackberry phone one last time, rubbed my belly, and disappeared into the night dressed to impress.

I was livid and if all these strangers weren't in my house, I would've acted a fool. But I let him go. I let Lionel go emotionally months ago when I realized he would never be my husband, and the best he could be was a good dad to I'yanna. I knew one day I would somehow be out of this situation and free from this overwhelming frustration.

Another pain ripped through my pelvis, overwhelming me in pain. I braced myself against the bed and continued to clutch the phone until the plastic squeaked against my hands. This pain was not regular pain. I knew this pain. This was a contraction. I huffed as the pain continued to surge through me so violently the skin on my arms tightened.

My body was telling me it was preparing for I'yanna. However, it had told me three times that week when I ended up in the emergency room and sent home for false labor. Unfortunately, every time I thought it was *time*, there was no dilation. I would get an IV, an excruciating cervical check, and sent home to rest.

Part of me thought that this could be another false alarm, but regardless these pains were hitting me hard. She was due any day and I was so tired of being pregnant. I was that big, waddling I could barely sit, breath or move pregnant. I was at the stage of help me get up, push me up the steps and help me prop my swollen feet up pregnant. My body frame was ready for the relief from the weight I'd gained.

My mood was foul, especially dealing with Lionel. Most women glowed and looked adorable pregnant. While all my friends, coworkers, and family said I did, all I could see was my full puffy face and swollen legs and feet.

Ready to have my body back was an understatement. I had just reached my goal weight and I was ready to get back in the gym and get back to where I was.

But there was no regret in choosing Iyanna and always being a mom first. Even knowing for at least 18 years, I'd have to put up with her dad's foolishness, she was a blessing.
The pain shot through me again and I knew my night would end with another trip to good old Gateway Hospital, or Gateway to Hell as the locals referred to it, sigh.

As the ravaging pain subsided, I made a slow shuffle toward the bathroom to take a shower. I peeked into AJ's room and he was sleeping like a little angel. I stared for a second as the light from the hallway fell across his innocent little face and smiled.

He was so busy and sweet. I loved this 4-year-old little boy with all my heart. He was a self-proclaimed "big boy" now, but his little chubby cheeks were still apparent, and he was still my baby. He was excited about being a big brother and told me all his plans. His logic was so funny, and I loved talking to him. I smiled and I quietly closed the door.

I shuffled to the restroom and retreated into the shower. The hot water streamed on me and was welcoming to my aching back. I could feel myself starting to panic and my emotions rising. I stuck my face into the streaming water to wash away the stress.

I couldn't deny the fact Lionel wasn't home was the source of my internal irritation and stress. It was eating at me even during the physical pain. I tried to stay calm and talk myself through what I needed to do for me and my baby. Sadly, in what should've been a peaceful, happy moment, I only felt anger and nagging disappointment that hadn't stopped for weeks. And it continued to worsen and was constantly reignited by Lionel's absence. He wasn't there now, and I feared he would never be there. I was still alone.

It reinforced that no matter what happened, I'd have to take care of myself and my baby. He did not have our backs.

He was about himself and his reckless life. He was not ready to be I'yanna's dad and this growing, thriving baby was not waiting for him to get ready.

The entire pregnancy had been deeply sad for me in so many ways. Each time I walked into the OB/GYN office alone, heard her heartbeat alone, saw her sonograms alone it was clear to me that I'd be raising her - alone. Lionel was already absent emotionally and seemed so uninterested in the birth of his first child. His behavior had become increasingly reckless. It was as if the pressure to be a man was closing in on him and he couldn't handle it. He was deflecting and had started denying that I'yanna was his child and accusing me of cheating.

I wanted to fight him and knock him out like Mayweather did de la Hoya earlier that night. It wasn't love that had me ready to hurt him; it was that feeling he always left me with at the end of the day... abandonment. I did not want I'yanna to experience that hallow, empty feeling I'd experienced from my biological dad.

It was a blatant disrespect for me, for my feelings, for us. It was a slap in the face knowing that he was selfish, and he didn't care about me or our family. He was a habitual cheater. A liar and a drunk. I knew. He knew it. His family knew it, but somehow everyone had bigger dreams for Lionel. Everyone except... well, Lionel.

But what did I expect? I don't know. I guess I just believed he could be a better man and that having his first child would make him more mature and man-up. But the opposite had occurred and the closer he got to fatherhood the more he retreated.

Family. I had a family. I had a husband. Maybe I don't deserve one. Maybe this is the retribution for my decisions. This is what I always told myself on days like this. I always convinced myself that this is the life I chose and somehow the guilt made sense and helped me push through the turmoil and drama that came with loving Lionel Montgomery. This was the bed I made.

When I found out we were having a daughter, I cried. My tears were for a layered number of reasons, but the main one being that I would be raising her with a father who I knew deep down would fail her repeatedly, just as my father had failed me.

No matter what I'd hoped for, he'd shown me that even before she was in this world, there was no indication of him changing for the better, but I still really wanted him to.

Although he'd moved back in, I hadn't forgiven him. It was tense all the time. There were unspoken issues, anger, and irritation constantly. We were never in a good place. I was so exhausted from his shenanigans - from this cycle of disappointment. I couldn't even muster up the strength to focus on being pissed. My focus was on me and my kids. Point. Blank. Period.

I sighed and inhaled the steam and smell of fresh Dove soap and lathered up. The hot water was soothing. Until, the razor-sharp cramps snatched me straight out of my thoughts, and I grabbed the shower knob for support, turning it off simultaneously. I stood there shaking in pain, holding my lower stomach. The pain held me for what seemed like forever and was so sharp it took my breath away. I knew with the increased sharpness of the pain that it was time to go to Gateway.

I knew I needed to call Lionel again. As hardhearted as I wanted to be in that moment, I knew I had no family in town. He was it, sadly. I sat on my bed with my cell phone nearby and picked it up to call Lionel. I put it down in irritation. He wasn't going to answer, and it was going to make me livid. I couldn't deal with this. This was probably causing me stress and affecting my baby. I took a few deep breaths, closed my eyes and prayed to God.

"Please help me calm down," I prayed, rocking to soothe the dull pains.

I'd called his cell phone and sent multiple text messages that night. I knew he was sending me straight to his voicemail and ignoring my messages. I tried again to let him know I was having contractions and going to the hospital.

"This is Lionel. You know what to do… BEEP," his voicemail repeated. I hung up, rolling my eyes and slamming the phone onto the bed. I needed to get moving so I started to apply lotion and put my clothes on. I'd find my own way.

A light knock came at my bedroom door and I could hear Shante's voice. I'd almost forgotten she was here. I couldn't understand what she was saying so I threw on my robe and cracked my door.

"I'm about to head home," she said quietly from the dark hallway. "You good?"

"No," I said. "I hate to ask you, but can you drop me off at the hospital? I will give you some gas money."

"The hospital?" Shante's voice said as she tried to hide both concern and fear. "Do you think the baby is coming?"

"I don't know. I just know I'm having some horrible pains," I said.

"Wow. OK. No problem, of course I can drop you off," she said, pausing. "Do you need me to call Lionel?"

"I've already tried. I do need someone to watch AJ," I said.

Shante agreed to call a cousin who she knew would be trustworthy and get there fast. I threw last minute items haphazardly in my already packed bag. I dialed my Auntie Paulette's phone number.

The phone rang twice, and Aunt Paulette's voice soothed me instantly. She always cracked me up when I called late. She knew she was asleep but would try to sound like she wasn't. In Virginia, she was an hour ahead of me and it was late.

"Hey, baby, what you up to this late at night?" She asked.

"Getting ready to go to the hospital again," I said, my voice strained from the pains.

"What's wrong?!" She asked, her voice, now alert and rising with worry.

"Having contractions. I think I'yanna may be coming tonight," I said, my voice breaking with emotion. It's something about talking to your auntie when you feel like crying that just brings it out of you.

There was a pause. Aunt Paulette was about to ask and we both were just waiting for it. She knew a lot about Lionel and I's relationship. She knew how hard I had tried to make it work. She knew about Adrian and I filing for divorce. She knew how to give advice and not take my life personally like

Momma. Aunt Paulette had been married for a long time. She was the only one of my mom's sisters that in a sense did it "right."

I felt anytime I said anything about Lionel to Momma, I was immediately reminded that I'd divorced Adrian to settle for this *loser*.

Aunt Paulette would at least listen even if she didn't like how Lionel was. She knew why I wanted us to work in my own way and gave me advice and support to work through the hard times. She said she always prayed for me to have peace and clarity.

"Where's Lionel?" She finally asked matter of fact. She knew I was stubborn. She knew he'd cheated on me and we were recovering from a breakup not too long ago.

"I don't know, auntie. He's probably at his girlfriend's house or at the club, most likely drunk and ignoring my calls. I can't get him, but I don't have time to wait on him."

"Well Fairlen, you can't do this by yourself and he needs to be there. He needs to step up!" She emphasized.

My aunt asked for his phone number and I already knew she would blow his phone up as soon as we hung up. If she couldn't get him, I'd decided at that moment not to care and just focus on me and my baby.

When Shante's cousin arrived to care for AJ, I went outside and went to Shante's car. I closed the door, buckled up, and braced myself for the ride across town. The radio played on low, creating background noise. I rubbed my belly and said a little prayer in my head, asking God to help me get through whatever me and baby girl had to do to get through this night.

The green digital numbers on Shante's dashboard read a few minutes after midnight. Shante was doing what her cousin should've been doing and there was really nothing to discuss. I took a very short nap and a bump in the road woke me up. We were almost to the hospital.

"You OK?" Shante asked, breaking the silence.

"Yeah, I'm OK," I answered.

A missed call from Aunt Paulette lit up my phone.

We pulled into the emergency room parking lot and Shante pulled up to the emergency doors to let me out of the car.

"I'll bring your bags in," she said. "I'll be right in."

I waddled into the emergency room and to the registration window. Everything began to happen fast as they saw my humongous bump and my flushed face. They took me straight to labor and delivery triage to get my vitals after I told them my symptoms and how far along I was in my pregnancy.

The triage nurse helped me navigate my way into a wheelchair and whisked me to the elevator. My ringtone cut through the early morning quiet of the empty hospital hallways. It was Aunt Paulette. I picked up the phone and told her to hold on. I braced for a painful contraction, clenching my body in the wheelchair and holding one of the armrests. I needed to hurry and get to the labor and delivery wing to see what was going on.

With the phone up to my ear, I could hear Aunt Paulette fussing and praying out loud to God. She was upset. I knew it without her explaining, because many times I'd prayed in anger from the frustration after a phone call with Lionel.

I asked if I could call her back after I got to my room and got settled. A part of me didn't want to deal with it right then and a part of me was ready to know the foolishness I knew had occurred from talking to a drunk Lionel. It was just too much. I almost wished she hadn't even called him, because now she was upset. I knew I'd be upset. I just wanted to have I'yanna in a peaceful setting and bring this gift into the world with love surrounding her.

"Take it easy, Fairlen," she said before hanging up. "I love you. Don't worry it's going to be OK."

I felt blank as I held my belly and felt the small bumps underneath the wheelchair as it glided along the waxed hospital floors. It was about 12:45 a.m. and so quiet. The nurse transporting me made small chatter as we got on the elevator.

"Are you having a boy or a girl, mom?" She asked in her Tennessee drawl deep.

"A girl." I replied.

"Oh, girls are just the best. I have two!" She said, in a quite chipper voice for third shift.

The smell of bleach and antiseptic met me as I exited the elevator. The sound of beeps echoed the hallway as I was wheeled into an empty birthing room, neatly prepared for the arrival of my sweet girl. I was just nervous and sick now, and almost felt weak and nauseous.

"Do you have any visitors?" She asked, looking at me. I didn't know how to answer. I was alone but knew Shante was coming up with my bag soon. The nurse noticed me pondering and put no pressure on me to answer.

"Well, mom, if you do, let me know who and we will get them a visitor pass... OK?"

I shook my head knowing it was me, I'yanna and God who would get us through this process.

I'd been through this before with AJ. But I was blessed to have Momma to hold my hand, as Adrian was deployed. I'd faced childbirth without the father of my child before. I could do it again. It was a sad thought.

I put on the thin hospital gown that draped my tummy like a mini tent and crawled into the somewhat stiff, uncomfortable hospital bed. I adjusted the pillows and propped myself up. As I waited, I felt I'yanna stirring inside my belly. She'd already turned head down and was effaced for weeks.

A couple of nurses came in and started talking to me a mile a minute about the process. They took my blood pressure, started an IV, and then checked to see where I was in the labor process.

One nurse held my hand and seconds later, the other nurse let out a surprised, "OK, mom, you are doing great! Mom, you are in labor! You are about 4 to 5 centimeters dilated! How exciting? You're halfway there and we will be meeting that sweet girl sooner rather than later!"

She fixed my gown and helped me sit back up in the bed. I was hooked up to a monitor where I could hear I'yanna's heartbeat constantly and could see my contractions happening. The news shook me for some reason. It's like I thought I had more time to figure things out and maybe even subconsciously was waiting for Lionel to surprise me and show up for me, for us, for our baby. The thought that he wasn't coming set in.

I picked up the phone, said a quick prayer, and called Lionel's number. He'd never be able to say I kept him from seeing his child no matter how I felt about him. He wasn't going to answer, and I was thinking of the message I was going to leave on his voicemail.

"Hello!"

His voice came through the receiver loud, agitated, and as I suspected he'd been drinking. It was a certain tone when Lionel drank. It was like a whole other person appeared that was angry about everything. He'd curse like a sailor and was just an emotional and belligerent drunk.

"Lionel, it's Fairlen," I said.

"I know! What do you want?" He replied rudely.

"I'm at the hospital. I'm in labor," I said calmly.

"OK!?" He replied sarcastically as if I was interrupting him.

I took the phone off my ear immediately and prepared to press the end call button. He yelled my name a few times after noticing my silence. I put the phone back up to my ear and held my tongue.

"Lionel, are you coming up here or not?" I asked calmly.

"Man, I don't even know. Like... is she even mine for real? Like don't play with me right now? And tell your family to stop blowing up my phone. I don't got time for the (expletive) games, Fairlen..."

I hung up on him as he continued his rant. I seriously could not take another ignorant word out his mouth and I knew if I kept talking, I would find myself out the bed, pacing the room, and putting me and my baby in distress.

I wasn't totally surprised. He was being typical Lionel, playing the role of the irresponsible little boy who always crumbled under pressure and responsibility.

It'd be a lie if I said I wasn't incredibly hurt by his words. Why wouldn't he think the baby was his? It wasn't Adrian's and I'd been in a relationship with only him since we started dating seriously.

I'd left my freaking husband for this man and was being treated like trash. I knew it wasn't a fairytale type story, but I also knew I wasn't a bad person and didn't deserve to be treated so horribly.

My baby didn't deserve to be treated like this, denied, questioned… just like I had been.

I was so mad, one single tear rolled down my face and I quickly wiped it. I refused to cry over this man ever again. Refused!

All I could do was pray and this extreme calm blanketed over me. I knew too well the spirit of calm that God sets in your heart when you are about to have a baby. It's an indescribable feeling that marries the worst pain of your life with unspoken endurance. Simply put, it hurts, but somehow you don't die. This was deeper than that. I felt God reassuring me that I'd be safe and make it through it. That 'Yanna would be well. That he had us and he was *Our Father* who would sustain us through anything we faced. Hope hugged me and peace kissed me. I exhaled and joy arrived in my heart.

The blessing of childbirth not being a constant pain but staggering over time was both a blessing and a curse. Time waits for no one. Not even Lionel to learn to be a father.

I'yanna was going to be born tonight. My sweet pea was going to be in my arms by morning. The joy of her arrival sliced through the heartbreak if even for a moment. I couldn't wait to meet her. From all the ultrasounds and heartbeats I heard, I knew she was a sweet, gentle, little girl. Her strong kicks also let me know she was strong like her mom. I could not wait to hold her, dress her up and kiss her fat cheeks.

My phone vibrated and I saw Aunt Paulette was texting me. "You OK?"
I called her immediately and let her know I was in labor. She reassured me she'd stay on the phone with me and I wouldn't be alone. Then she told me what I'd figured. She had been able to get through to Lionel.

"Fairlen, that boy has some issues!" She said. I could tell she was trying to hold back some extreme annoyance and choice words.

"What happened?" I asked, tiredly. I knew if he talked to her like he'd talk to me. It was going to be classic.

"So... I called him a few times," she said. "Finally, he picked up. I could tell he was drunk because he was slurring his speech and talking extremely loudly. You were right, I could tell he was at the club because I could hear the music blaring in the background. He was yelling, 'Who the (expletive) is this? How did you get my (expletive) number!' All belligerent and ignorant."

"That sounds like him," I chimed in.

"I told him you were at the hospital. I said, 'Lionel you need to get there ASAP,'" she said. "This fool said, 'I don't know if that baby is mines!'" she mimicked.

I had already planned to get a DNA test as soon as she was born to shut him all the way up. I shook my head as she continued.

"Aunt Paulette, I'm not surprised. I don't even expect anything," I said.

"You don't deserve this mess, Fairlen. You are too smart, beautiful, and kind of a woman to put up with this bull! This is just too crazy," she said. "But don't worry you won't be alone. I'll stay on the phone with you and talk you through this. I'm right here with you. Just leave me on speaker."

Almost simultaneously, a small knock came at the door and Shante walked in with my bags. She waved, smiled, and sat my bags down on the couch area.

She asked me how I was doing and apologized for taking so long. She was shocked when I told her I was in labor already and would be getting my epidural shortly. She smiled with excitement and reassured me she'd stay with me.

In a blur, my door opened, and closed multiple times with nurses coming in and out, hooking me to this and that. I'yanna's loud strong heartbeat filled the room and zig zags coordinated my contractions across a monitor.

I continued through labor, contractions hitting me in waves, ebbing and flowing through my back and pelvis. I'd grip the side of my bed and let one pass. I breathed through them and then tried to weigh if it was bearable or if I needed drugs.

After a particularly painful contraction, I lay out of breath with my heart pounding. My face was flushed. I became overwhelmed and began to cry. I hit my nurses' button. When she arrived, I asked for my epidural and she turned me on my side and made sure I was comfortable to continue laboring until the anesthesiologist arrived.

Soon a needle was going in my back and I sat as still as I could as the pricks and pressure moved through my back and settled into the line into my back. Soon the numbness slipped down my stomach and embraced the pain in my pelvis and rested at my toes. The stabbing, wringing, cringing pangs of labor subsided eventually and my body relaxed. I could still feel the pressure of the cramps, but not the sharp pains. I was relieved and calm. I sucked on ice chips and rested. I finally could fully focus on I'yanna.

Aunt Paulette played a few gospel and worship songs over her phone and it further calmed me. During all the drama of my pregnancy my sweet baby had always been my calm. We'd been bonded since the day I got out of Adrian's car and determined I'd never take her life because I knew she'd be great no matter how she was conceived. She grew in my womb as I grew in my faith and determination to be a good mother.

I closed my eyes and rested for an hour. It was peaceful for the first time that night. Aunt Paulette said to call her when I woke up. When I woke up, I saw Shante talking on her phone in a hushed tone, gesturing emphatically. She walked over to my bedside and asked how I was feeling.

"I'm doing good," I said. "Just sleepy. What time is it?"

"It's almost 3 a.m.," Shante said.

"So…. Fairlen, my grandma just called me and told me Lionel showed up at her house about an hour ago. He'd got from the club and I told her you were in labor and needed to talk to him because he needs to be here. She convinced him to come up here. He will be here in a few minutes. I just wanted to let you know."

I thanked her and then asked Aunt Paulette who'd rejoined us if she heard her.

"He's coming up there!?" Aunt Paulette asked. "OK. Lord help us all!"

I had no real emotion at that moment. I wasn't happy, sad, mad, or anything. I was tired. I was ready to meet my baby. I had a mission and my mind was blocked off from anyone and anything except getting I'yanna here healthy.

I looked up at Shante from the bed. She was reading my face to see if I was mad. I wasn't. Had she overstepped? Not really, I knew she wanted her cousin to do what's right and she was in an odd situation.

"Thanks again for letting me know, Shante. Thanks for everything," I said, with a weak smile.

She returned to the couch in the corner and I again watched my monitor relay contractions as I rested. I was so tired in so many ways.

My eyes popped open as I heard shoes clacking up the waxed hallways. I knew the sound of those shoes and that hard walk. Those expensive shoes he couldn't afford. The ones that walked out the kitchen hours ago to go get liquor and never returned. The ones that probably danced with multiple women in the club or slowed dance with the ex-girlfriend he really loved.

Lionel walked in the room still wearing what I'd last seen him in when he left his fight party except, he looked very disheveled.

He walked up to my bed and the smell of cognac preceded him. He smelled like a whole fifth of liquor. My eyes did not leave him as he approached me. I just stared and said nothing.

The peace I felt, fled the room with his presence. Shante broke the silence and came over to talk to Lionel.

"Congratulations, cousin!" She said, hugging him.

"For what?" Lionel said, still inebriated. "I don't even know if this baby...."

He started and I interrupted, unleashing an extremely loud "Shut up!" and pointing my finger in his face. It was so abrupt, it offended me. My blood boiled at that point; I couldn't even contain the immediate rage I felt. The awkwardness sliced through the air and the tension exploded.

"I'm so sick of you saying that because you don't want to step up and be a father. So, if you don't just shut up, you can get out. You don't have to be here!" I said, my voice rising with my anger. "I got here without you and I'll be just fine having *my daughter* without you too. You're drunk anyways and I don't want that around my child!!!"

The way I erupted, that had been on my heart and I had no more patience or calm left for Lionel. He was not going to come in here and ruin such a special occasion.

Aunt Paulette chimed in and Shante chastised and tried to quiet Lionel, as he began gesturing and yelling back at me and calling me names. His male cousin who'd driven him there grabbed his shoulders and held him back.

I could feel my face getting hot and I'd sat up the part of my body I could feel and began gesturing at him, too. Everyone was yelling. I don't even remember what I was saying but was letting him know he could kick rocks. I was hurt deep down. This was supposed to be a beautiful family moment, but it wasn't. It was rowdy, turmoil-filled and tense. This was not the way to bring a baby into the world.

It was not how AJ entered the world. He was surrounded by the love of me and my mom. I did not fear anything, especially not abandonment, anger or accusatory threats. It was nothing but love.

This was not love.

My monitors began to chime as my heart rate and blood pressure increased. The commotion brought a couple of nurses rushing through the door of my room.

One of the nurses was a 'don't play no games' type of nurse. She looked at Lionel with a very stern look. Then turned to me and said bluntly, "Everything with you has been perfect all night, but your blood pressure has increased greatly, and I'm concerned you and the baby are being stressed." She then turned to Lionel and said in a serious tone, "Sir, if you are causing her and the baby stress then you don't need to be here. But that is *your* decision.

"Either you are going to be here to help her as she has this beautiful baby, *or* we can call security, and have you escorted out immediately for causing her and the baby too much harm!" She didn't crack a smile and her words were crisp and clear. "Again, that's *your* choice."

It seems the deep breath she took, siphoned in some of the strong smell of alcohol that was emitting from Lionel.

She turned to me and asked me if I wanted him there and if not, she could easily make him leave by calling security.

I could hear Aunt Paulette agreeing loudly on the phone with some emphatic "Mmm, hmmm!" and "That's right."

There was a quiet pause as everyone looked at me for an answer. Lionel was acting nonchalant, looking down at his phone, and shrugging his shoulders, mumbling that it was "whatever." I was thoroughly aggravated.

I think at that moment I really understood the gravity of what I was about to endure for at least the next 18 years of my life. It was clear that when things got real, he was going to try everything to get out of it and *trying* to make him do the right thing was not possible.

While aggravated, a part of me still wanted the father for I'yanna, to at least, be given a chance to be there. I wanted her to have the chance I never had and that was to know him, form her own opinions, and have memories of him in her life.

The fact he was trying to deny her cut me so deep because I knew that feeling to my core. I knew the feeling of your father looking at you, turning his face, and riding off into the sunset with his *real family*. I didn't want I'yanna to feel that ever in her life, even if her father was Lionel. I still had this deep affection for Lionel and thought maybe having a child could bring out something in him that he needed to heal, grow, and be better.

I know AJ had changed me at that time in my life. I held out an ounce of hope. I knew I'yanna was extremely special before she was born and if anyone could save him, she could. I knew she was meant to change the world that day.

I told the nurse he was alright to stay and shot him a look that said, "I will have you kicked out if you act a fool."

Lionel walked to the hospital window and stared out at the darkness dotted with streetlights and business signs. Shante and his other cousin followed and talked to him. A few minutes later they all said they were going to get some coffee and something to eat. The brain fog from the epidural caused everything after that to become a blur as I woke from my nap to faces around me.

"Wake up, mom," a nurse said. "We need to get you set up!"

"Alright, mom, you are ready to push!" Another nurse chimed in.

I was groggy, confused, and trying to take in everything all at once.

Already!? I thought. "It's time!?" I asked as I realized that it was actually *time*.

I looked to my left and there was a nurse. I looked to my right, and saw a sober, somewhat terrified Lionel. He looked sleepy, somewhat excited, and extremely terrified like he had never taken sex education and didn't know what to expect. It was his first child, so I knew he was freaking out and truly had never experienced childbirth. I was in a fog as I shook off the sleepiness and blinded by the lights that were quickly turned on in the room.

It was a commotion and it seemed like a million people were in my room. A whole gang of nurses rolled in a mobile nursery. The excitement, the chatter, everything filled the room and I realized it was truly time to meet my baby.

My mind swirled and I talked to God in my head and tried to listen to the instructions. My legs were propped up for me and everyone began talking to me at once. Beyond my blanketed legs I pushed, pushed, breathed and pushed some more. There was a ton of pressure and I felt my body shifting below. I heard the gasps and chatter of the doctor and nurses. I felt Lionel grasping my hand tightly and his eyes were huge.

"Come on, mom, she's almost out!" The doctor said.

I felt extreme pressure as I'yanna made her entrance into the world and I pushed her to pass her shoulders.

"You're doing great, mom. Her head is out, let's push a little more!"

The excitement filled the air as her body slipped out on this side of life. My body shook as I pushed her. My head hurt from pushing and focusing so hard. There was this wave of exclamations among the staff. They suctioned her little mouth and she let out a loud cry.

It was a blur and time rushed and stood still at the same time. I was exhausted and tried to focus on seeing my daughter. The nurses clapped in excitement with so much glee exclaimed over how pretty she was and how much hair she had.

"Mom, you have a perfect baby girl!" A nurse said.

"5:40 a.m.," The doctor said as a nurse charted the stats. "Let's get her weight and length."

They held her little face up so I could see her. My heart melted as I saw her headful of dark hair and fat cheeks peek at me quickly. She was gorgeous. Then they whisked her to the side to give her a quick wipe down, take her weight and measurements.

I was pushed and prodded on to finish the birthing process. I wanted to hold her as I heard the nurses continue to dote over her. Lionel was in the nurse's way like an excited dad snapping pictures with his phone. His voice was full of love and excitement.

My heart melted again. Maybe I'yanna was brought here to change Lionel. The way he was looking at her and really involved in this process gave me a second of hope.

I'yanna was his first child, his only child, and when I told him I was pregnant his reaction had been very lackluster, skeptical, and doubtful. He seemed to have no doubt at this moment.

I could hear his voice rising as he talked about her hair and her cheeks.

I wanted to see my baby!

Finally, after what seemed like forever, they brought I'yanna over to me. The moment she was put into my arms I literally fell in love with my little mama.

"Hello there, sweet girl, mommy has been dying to meet you!" I said, kissing her little face and cuddling her to my chest. She was so warm and cooed softly. Her eyes were shut tight and when she eventually opened them, they were big, beautiful brown eyes full of kindness. She was a precious baby. I was so in love with my baby girl. She had a head full of dark long hair for an infant. Everything she did was so cute. She sucked on her fingers loudly and everyone awed.

The nurse asked me if I wanted to do skin-to-skin or breastfeed and I told the nurses I did but was really, really tired.

"Dad, do you want to hold her and feed her while mom gets a little rest?" The nurse asked, coming to take I'yanna from my arms. I nodded, yes, as she looked to me for my approval. I was exhausted from all the pushing and focusing, sweating and praying.

I watched as the nurse placed I'yanna in Lionel's arms. He was overjoyed and smiling so big his cheeks looked like they would burst.

"Come here, lil' mama," he said, receiving her little swaddled body into his arms. "Come to daddy, pretty girl. You are so beautiful and perfect. You are daddy's princess."

I looked over at them and was honestly shocked. The man who denied her just a few hours ago, was all in. He snapped photos of I'yanna and selfies posing with her to post on social media.

We spent the day taking turns holding I'yanna, taking phone calls, sending photos, and enjoying new life. She was just so amazing and sweet. I wanted to hold her every second.

Lionel became distracted and at some point, I noticed he was on his phone and ignoring calls. Every few minutes I'd hear his phone ring and he would ignore the call. Finally, he answered it and he did it right in front of me.

It was the ex-girlfriend he was in love with. It was the same girl that I found out he'd cheated on me with while I was pregnant.

Before I could get mad at the utter disrespect of this hussy calling and him answering it, what he said stopped me in my tracks. I could hear her speaking loudly even though his phone was not on speaker.

"Lionel, where are you? Where did you go? You just left me at the club!"

He apologized to her. *What?* I thought. He never apologized – to anyone. He really liked her, I guess.

"Why are you ignoring my calls, Lionel? I was so worried about you? Where are you? And who is this baby in the picture!?" She continued asking, almost sounding like she was crying.

Aww... she really loved him. I thought to myself.

"Look, Fairlen had my baby tonight." He told her, looking over at me. I knew he was saying all this so I could hear it. I rolled my eyes but listened. "I really want to try and make it work with Fairlen and I want to be in my daughter's life. She deserves both her parents and I just want to man-up and do what's right."

I could hear the girl crying and she hung up the phone. I almost felt pity for her because she, too, had believed the future Lionel spoke of with her and didn't realize he had no way of living up to any of the promises.

I also felt a bit of glee. She knew about me; knew I was pregnant, and still slept with my man, and he'd chosen me and our daughter in the end. Checkmate.

"Why did you send a picture of my baby to your girlfriend?" I asked drowsily and sarcastically.

"She's not my girlfriend and I needed her to know I wasn't playing games, Fairlen." He said seriously. He looked down at I'yanna adjusting her pacifier and then looked at me. "I don't want anyone else raising my daughter. I'll never let another man raise her. I'm her daddy and always will be. I don't want her to grow up like I did without both my parents. Fairlen, I won't let what happened to me happen to her. I swear I won't."

He was tearing up, rocking her back and forth in the dim lit hospital room. I could tell he was still coming off a mean hangover but also, he meant it. While I didn't know everything he'd been through, I knew it was traumatic and bad. I knew his childhood trauma was why he drank and why he hurt.

I assured him I didn't want her to grow up like I did either with my dad denying me and I didn't want to struggle as a single mother. It was the first time in months we'd talked about our relationship and as awkwardly timed as it was, it was right on time.

The birth of I'yanna had been a turning point in his life and seeing me give birth was both traumatic and magical for him. The few glimpses I got of him as I gave birth made me want to laugh and cry because I'd never seen him so happy and terrified all at the same time. The funny person he was had so many facial expressions when I thought about it later.

Deep down, I cared deeply about Lionel and wanted so much for his life. I'd just been hurt in the process of wanting to fix him and it'd jaded and calloused me to him.

In this moment, the affection I felt for him surged as I watched him hold his daughter. Maybe it was postpartum hormones, but I found myself tearing up as he sang to her and put all his attention into her. He seemed truly happy being a dad to I'yanna.

Despite that feeling, when the sun came up, I made an appointment at a DNA testing center to have someone come to the house and have I'yanna and Lionel tested.

He'd never again doubt if she was his. I wouldn't let him be able to say for the next 18 years, "I don't know if she's mine." The test came back positive and for some time Lionel was deeply in love with life with I'yanna, AJ, and me.

But the joy of being a new father did not change the dynamic between Lionel and me. After I'yanna's birth one thing quickly became apparent, we could not stay together and to be good parents we needed to do it separately.

Chapter 16

The Escape

The orange scrubs smelled of cheap, almost sweaty detergent and my skin itched at the thought of how many bodies had donned this suit.

The deputy barked commands at several female inmates and I was ushered towards a room where I knew my exposure would begin. This blanket of humiliation enveloped me. We entered a bright room where a camera stood with a pale blue background where my mugshot would be taken. It felt like being at the DMV but I felt 10 times worse about this picture. I turned to the left. I faced the front and then I turned to the right. With each click and flash, the depth of where I was sunk in.

This man had put me in jail. I was in shock and disbelief. I held my composure in each shot. I know my face showed my anger and disappointment, and though my emotions were as heavy as the angry tears I was holding back, I could not show any weakness. If I did, he would have won.

I was drained and emotionally empty from all the lies, all of the deceit, and all of the craziness that had been created in this facade of a relationship with Lionel. I tried to uphold the wall, but I was at my wits ends. This day, I knew it over indefinitely. Never again. I was done.

Other women followed me. I didn't make eye contact. I looked down and kept moving. I know it was jail and not prison but, in the moment, it felt so permanent all of a sudden.

They rolled my fingers across a black ink pad and onto boxes of a fingerprint sheet, permanently putting my identity into the legal system. I was led down the long gray concrete halls of the Montgomery County Jail to a holding cell. They explained I would be there for 12 hours, to "cool off."

How could I cool off when I didn't do anything violent to be here? The arresting officer had explained that I had been charged with domestic assault as he handcuffed me and put me in the back of the patrol car in front of my home just hours earlier. The look in his eyes showed regret and almost dismay as he knew I was telling him the truth when I pleaded my innocence. But in a domestic situation someone is going to jail, and Lionel was convincing when he called 911 and screamed, I had pulled a knife on him and tried to stab him the night prior.

All lies. We had argued and I'd left. It hurt to the core that he'd come up with an elaborate plot to get back at me. But finally, this was the wakeup call I needed that showed me how far he'd go to, not only hurt me, but destroy me.

I was going to call Momma, but I knew my sister, Iris had called her and told her because she was there and was able to take custody of I'yanna when I was arrested. Iris was my oldest sister on my dad's side who had moved to Clarksville after Hurricane Katrina.

This was going to be a long 12 hours.

The slam of that heavy steel door is real, sickening sound. I felt trapped like a caged animal. The smell of desperation and funk filled the air. It was mostly quiet. None of the cat calling like in the movie. I sat on the stiff, thin mattress, and stared blankly in disbelief. I felt shattered, broken, and mortified.

Calming my chaotic thoughts was a struggle. I needed to be numb to face this strange place. Time started to go in slow motion without the luxury of a clock. I stared at the walls riddled with the graffiti of broken women. Messages of love, hate, and time were etched on the white brick walls from women also looking for an answer to why they were in such a trapped predicament. We all wanted to explain.

I felt disconnected. I was not one of these women. I knew why I was here, and it wasn't my fault. Yet, like these women, with their inked-out revelations, I'd hit a new low by being in this small cell.

Momma understood the situation and how I got to where I was. She never liked Lionel and she'd told me to leave so many times. The dread of disappointing her hung heavy over me. If Momma had said nothing else to us, she preached to us, "I won't be visiting any of my children through a glass window" and to know that allowing this situation to get this far weighed on me.

I remember hearing all of the warnings that Momma had preached to me over the time. I had become so blinded by

Lionel with what I thought was love, I didn't realize I was attempting to fix his broken pieces that were unable to be put back together.

While sitting in the cell, I etched my own revelation on my heart's wall, "Leave and never look back. Lionel and nobody else is worth being in jail."

After I'yanna's birth, Lionel and I were off and on as he continued to see his ex-girlfriend. I'yanna was about five months old, and while the joy and light she exuded created beautiful moments, the toxicity of Lionel and I was affecting everything.

We were both living separate lives although we were residing under one roof. Neither of us were naive to believe that we were being monogamous in the relationship. I don't know why we wouldn't leave the relationship. We attempted to be respectful with one another, but it was clear we both were unfaithful.

I had finally told Lionel that I wanted out and did not want to live with him any longer. I had been actively looking for a place for my children and I to live and begun the process of moving out. In his anger, Lionel did not make this an easy process. I never said I would stop him from being a father, but it was like the thought of me taking I'yanna to live with me drove him to some dark place.

I later learned the level of deception and betrayal Lionel had stooped to in effort to get full custody of I'yanna. His plot to have me arrested was just the first step in his plan.

It was a Friday in September 2007, and that evening my nephew had a football game that I'yanna and I were going to attend and afterwards I had plans to go out with friends.

As I was packing her bags and getting ready to go, Lionel started arguing with me about him not knowing where I was taking I'yanna. I purposely ignored him and refused to answer his questions. My silence infuriated him, and he was in my face yelling. He then put his hands on me and pushed me into a corner. I immediately shoved him away from me and the argument escalated. I quickly grabbed I'yanna and her things and left for the night. I was not planning to return that night. It was not uncommon for us to have arguments and one leave and come back the next day as if nothing happened.

The next morning, I picked up I'yanna from the babysitter. As I pulled into the driveway, Lionel's van was backed up to the front door and all of I'yanna's clothes, toys and belongings were packed up in his van. I immediately said to myself he wasn't taking my baby anywhere. I proceeded to unlock the door and it jarred due to the chain lock being latched. I worked my hand through the door to try to get in and yelled for him to let me in. I could hear his voice.

"She's back. Can you send someone out?" He said to the dispatcher.

Lionel let me in, and I asked him what was going on, and why he was packing I'yanna's things. I couldn't believe him, where did he think he was taking my child?

When Clarksville Police arrived several minutes later, an officer pulled me to the side to explain the situation. My heart was beating out my chest as I put it all together and saw what Lionel was trying to do. He was trying to get me out of the picture so he could take my daughter.

I don't play about my kids. I'm always a mom first and due to Lionel's irresponsible behavior I didn't trust him to have my daughter for long periods of time. We'd had an agreement that he could keep her while I worked during the week and on some weekends, but beyond that I did not want my daughter with him long-term.

The officer explained there was a warrant for my arrest from the night before because Lionel claimed that I had pulled a knife on him. The officer stated that Lionel was never able to produce the so-called knife in question. However, due to state law he had to arrest someone because it was a domestic claim. When it was determined that I would be arrested, I called for my sister to come and get I'yanna.

Lionel of course objected and said that he wanted to take his daughter. I told the officer that Lionel was not on her birth certificate because he refused to sign it and I was the only "legal" guardian. As her legal guardian, I wanted her to be with my sister, Iris.

The officer, who also seemed to see right through what was going on, agreed and said that I would have the sole right to decide where my daughter went. He was very understanding and reassuring. He knew that I was not guilty of what I was accused of so when he brought me before the magistrate, he told me he'd ask for a low bond.

Sitting in that cold, small jail cell, I'd never felt so alone and humiliated. As I reflected, I realized then that there was no extent that Lionel would not go to. He was determined to get what he wanted even if that meant my demise. I had been sleeping with the enemy.

There was nothing left to say, and I leaned on my support system to get me and my children away from this vindictive man once I was released from jail.

Momma came to my rescue. She bonded me out of jail and then stayed to help me escape this daunting situation. Within the week, I had us a new apartment to live in and knew I was in for a fight with a broken, spiraling man. She stayed for one month helping me get on my feet. She helped me get set up in my own house and made sure me and the kids were comfortable. She always wanted to be sure that I understood I did not need a man to survive. I could do it on my own just as she had for us three girls.

Lionel had gone to a local attorney trying to obtain full custody of I'yanna after my arrest. He lied and said that he had no way of contacting me and was petitioning for full legal custody of our daughter. He knew very well where I lived, and we were in contact as he had her every other weekend.

I did not know the level of his desperation. I had not indicated I would not let him be a father to I'yanna, but maybe his demons led him to lash out and try to destroy me and everything he loved in the process.

One morning my cell phone rang around 5 a.m., when I saw Lionel's name, I declined the call. It was a Sunday morning and it was my day set aside to be with my family. I did not have time for whatever foolishness he had going on.

I saw he left a message, so I reluctantly played the message as I got up and started to prepare for church that morning.

Lionel's voice was slurred as he pleaded and said that he "wanted his family back" and could not live life knowing that another man could be raising his daughter. He sounded like he'd been crying and was asking me to forgive him for everything that had occurred. I deleted the message and went along with my day. I was never going back.

Monday, Lionel showed up at my house unannounced to talk to me. Against my better judgment I decided to allow him to speak his peace. He apologized nonstop for falsely filing the police report and said he had called the District Attorney's office multiple times to try to have my domestic assault case dismissed. They would not allow him to. I recall him saying he was just in over his head and he never expected things to turn out like "this."

I listened to him speak, but his pleas fell on deaf ears. We were not getting back together no matter what he said. What he did to the mother of his child was a wrong that he could not undo and showed me all I needed to know. The only thing we needed to discuss was the best way to co-parent and do what's best for I'yanna.

I wanted to be on amicable terms with Lionel because I wanted I'yanna to know and love her father, but I wasn't willing to risk my freedom to do it. I wasn't the kind of mom who bashed her child's father because I didn't like him. I wanted her to have a relationship with her dad.

I wanted her to know her dad and respect him and possibly have what I never had growing up, a close relationship with her daddy. In a way, I strived for her to be a daddy's girl. I knew even if Lionel was a poor significant other, maybe he could be a great dad if he tried.

But it seemed life was swallowing him up and Lionel was spiraling. I didn't want to be a part of his self-destruction and I saw quickly he was willing to take any and everyone down with him to get his way.

Chapter 17

An Unimaginable Act

December 7, 2007

I stretched out in my king size bed as the sun slipped its rays through my curtains.

"Whew!" I said, letting out a huge yawn and stretching my limbs. Gazing at my alarm clock, I realized my sleeping-in had only been one extra hour from my regular early rise.

I heard I'yanna on the baby monitor making baby noises and cooing. At seven months old, she was all gums and slobbery smiles and I just loved seeing her grin. I watched the monitor, and she was sitting up, baby babbling, and cuddling a stuffed toy.

"Ta ta ta ta, da da da, brrrr brrr," she said cheerfully, loving the sound of her own voice and the feel of her little lips vibrating with spit bubbles.

I smiled at the sound of my baby "talking." She always had a lot to say. I could watch her all day. I smiled and prepared to go get all the baby snuggles and sugars from my *fat momma*. This was my favorite part of my day, seeing my sweet girl so happy to see me in the morning.

I'd been hustling so hard to make extra Christmas money. My boss, Kristie, who I butt heads with often because we had a different way of seeing things, had asked me to take the morning off since I'd had so much overtime. I think she thought I would push back, but I was tired and hit her with a cheerful "OK." It was good not running out of the house, rushing AJ and 'Yanna to daycare, or dropping 'Yanna off with her dad on his weekends.

He'd asked to watch her for the weekend and while we weren't on the best of terms, I didn't want to stop him from being a father. I wanted them to have a bond and let her decide how she saw him when she was old enough.

Lionel seemed to try to be a better man when he was in the role of father. The way he played with her, making goofy faces and throwing her up in the air. Hearing how she'd laugh with him was so heartwarming. Her grandfather and great-grandmother spoiled and adored Lionel's only child. They were enablers of his destructive behavior, but I knew if it came to it they'd make sure I'yanna wanted for nothing. I got I'yanna ready to go to her father's.

The chaotic life of being a single mom was running me ragged, and this much needed morning break was so refreshing. I opened the door to I'yanna room and saw her sitting up in her crib. She'd found her pacifier and was chewing on it and chilling. "What chu' talking about fat mama!?" I said, reaching for her soft chubby arms. She smiled big exposing her gums as I brought her round cheeks to my lips and covered them with kisses.

"Hey, 'Yanna Pooh!! 'Yanna Pooh!!" I said, dancing with her in my arms.

She replied with a "Dadadadadada."

"No, say MaMa!" I said laughing and carrying her to her furry white carpet where she made her way in a swift crawl to her toys. At seven months old she was alert and busy and had hit all her milestones.

I sat her down and went through her closet full of clothes and picked out a cute jean outfit. When it came to dressing I'yanna I had a shopping addiction. She had clothes for days, most still new with tags. Her closet was full of clothes on tiny pink hangers. All of the dresses were color coded and organized by size.

I, like my mom, made sure my kids were dressed the best even if I had to sew my clothes together, so to speak.

I'yanna's looked adorable in her flared blue jeans and matching jean jack. I picked out some cute pink barrettes for her hair.

"You're going to look so cute when you see your daddy today!" I said.

After giving her a bath and making sure she smelled of baby lotion and powder, I dressed her, chatting with her like we were besties.

"You're going to have fun, 'Yanna Banana!" I sang looking into her bright eyes. She smiled. I cuddled her neck and planted more kisses on her. She thought mommy was so funny and we had such a sweet bond. Having a daughter was the best! It was like having your own baby doll to dress up.

"Yes, girl," I said, pulling her to her feet and bouncing her little body on my legs. "You are looking ca-ute. You are the cutest baby in town," I said, chatting with her. By this time, AJ had woken up and popped into the living room.

"Good morning, sleepyhead!" I said to him. He came to me for a hug and then brought his face so close to I'yanna, their noses touched and 'Yanna gabbed as her slightly uncoordinated flailing arms found their way to his face a few times.

He pretended to be hurt with a big dramatic "Ow!" and she smiled big, with drool rolling down her little chin.

"It's not funny, Yaya!" He said jokingly to her. She was always happy.

I looked at the time and saw that just that fast an hour had passed. I went through the day's events in my head. I needed to drop I'yanna to Lionel, get to lunch with my friend, and meet Adrian so he could pick up AJ for the weekend. It was the dads' weekend and my weekend off work. I had some time for self-care and rest, a rarity.

While I'd miss my babies, I could get some Christmas shopping done, catch up on some shows, nap, organize the house a little, and just do me for a second. I looked at my nails. *I may get a polish change and a pedicure*, I thought.

"Come on AJ, we have to get going, you know your dad is picking you up this afternoon," I said.

"Yay!" He said, spontaneously leaping up and running out some of that 4-year-old energy that seemed never-ending. He had so much energy and was always running everywhere.

"Stop running and go to the bathroom so I can wash you up," I yelled.

Everything was packed and by the door for both kids. I ran down the list in my head: bottles, formula, more diapers, clothes… check.

I must say, while my mom had a little OCD while we were growing up, it had rubbed off on me. It had created a way of living that kept me grounded. All the dread in pre-planning, always cleaning and order that I complained about as a child, in an odd turn of events was something I was proud of. It made life simple to live in order. It kept my brain in line with my life.

AJ was being a typical boy getting distracted and doing jumping kicks in the hallway. I told him to go brush his teeth and gazed at the clock again.

The morning was going fast, but I was pacing myself.

"Alright, mama let's get this hair in order," I said, smelling her soft hair.

She was born with the curliest, blackest, and thickest hair and it'd only gotten longer and thicker. I loved her hair and I wanted to raise her to love her hair too. I gently moisturized and combed her hair, gathered two little pigtails, and clipped them into two pink and blue barrettes. I chatted busily reassuring her I'd have her hair looking fabulous.

I propped I'yanna on the couch and put a pillow on both sides as she watched TV. She held her bottle up like an expert and watched the furry red muppet bounce across the screen. I moved methodically through the morning getting myself dressed, AJ washed and dressed, and everyone fed. Soon we were all calmly walking out the door and heading to Foster's Funeral Home to meet Lionel.

When I pulled up, Lionel was sitting in his van. I felt my body tense up and took a deep breath as I pulled my car about 10 feet from his van. I was hoping for as little interaction as possible.

He got out and sauntered to my car. I could hear him singing the hymn, "I'll Fly Away,"

I'll fly away, Oh, glory, I'll fly away; (in the morning). When I die, Hallelujah, by and by, I'll fly away (I'll fly away).

He was always humming and singing. I unstrapped the baby. I kissed her cheeks and told her I'd see her in a few days. Lionel took 'Yanna from my arms and proceeded to strap her into his van. I jumped back in the car, running from the nip of the cold winter. We barely looked at each other.

I blared the heat and rubbed my hands together. As he got in the van, I looked on my front floorboard and saw he forgot her baby bag. I honked my horn and yelled out the window, "Hey, you didn't get her bag!" He jogged over to the car to get the bag.

Lionel popped his head in the window to get the bag and looked in the backseat to speak to AJ.

"Hey, lil' man," he said. "Remember, AJ, I always loved you."

I thought it was an odd thing to say. AJ smiled as Lionel looked at him through the window before walking back to the van. I felt the annoyance bubbling up in me. He was always kind to AJ, but not a good example as to how to conduct himself as a man.

He had used the kids to guilt me about us not being a family and I felt he was doing it again. He always spoke about having both his parents and how that could've changed his life. In his head, it was my fault we weren't a family. I remained silent and looked ahead before driving towards the restaurant to have lunch with my friend.

AJ smacked on French fries and smiled happily. He was such a cool kid. It was nice to spend some time with just us for a minute. I made conversations asking him what's his favorite this and that was and laughed at him.

Adrian showed up soon after he finished his meal and we did the hand-off. We were cordial and I'd taken the news of his fiancé well. I knew good co-parenting was possible because Adrian and I did it well. I kissed AJ and said bye as he jumped in his dad's car and they drove off.

He's Gone

By 1 p.m., I was at my desk looking at the stack of work that sat before me. I was going to dive into it and get it done this Friday afternoon. My co-workers and I made small talk as a couple of customers trickled in here and there.

It was just four of us there and we'd all become cool in the time I'd worked there. Yet, as it sometimes is working with women, there was a level of pettiness and cattiness often led by our boss. I wasn't about all that. I just wanted to work, collect my coins, and take care of me and my kids. I didn't have time for all the extra drama. I stayed cordial as the only woman of color and kept it pushing.

As I logged my work into the computer, my phone rang.

There are moments in your life where one thing changes everything and this phone call was the moment that altered the course of my day and my life forever.

"Hello, this is Fairlen. How can I help you?" I said, in my professional voice.

There was a pause and I heard a man clear his throat and it seemed he was trying to gain his composure.

"Fairlen…" The man said, his voice cracking and shaking with emotion. "Fairlen, he's gone!"

I tried to catch the voice. My face scrunched in bewilderment.

"Excuse me!?" I said, in confusion. "Who is this?"

My professionalism had gone out the window as I listened to this man weeping on the phone with such emotion and grief.

"He's gone!" He repeated. "Lionel's … dead."

The words rang in my ear like a sick echo and my heart literally thumped in utter terror. I felt my skin turn cold and it felt like I was watching myself as I literally screamed out loud. My hands began shaking and I almost dropped the receiver.

"Dead? I just saw him! What happened? Was there a car accident? Where's my baby?"

I felt I was silent but in reality, I was frantic.

"No... Noooo!" I screamed and everyone in the room, customers included stared at me. They knew something awful was happening and it stopped everyone in their tracks. I could feel a co-worker touching me and holding me, as everything began to spin out of control.

"What happened!? Where's my baby?!" I yelled into the phone, tears bursting out of my face. I was trying to regain control to assess the situation, but my mind was racing from shock. I couldn't hear from my own fervor of a conglomeration of emotions all battling my nerves and brain to find conclusions and answer questions and make sense of such a shocking statement.

"Where's I'yanna?!" I screamed over and over into the receiver. "Lionel had I'yanna, where is she?"

The man on the other end, was Lionel's barber who I knew well. He was crying.

"I don't know, I don't know," he said emphatically.

I was having an out of body experience. Like the world just deflated right around my body. Like I'd melted into some strange dimension and I was a stranger in my own existence. Nothing made sense.

"Lionel's dead," is the only thought that I could come up with. *Where is my baby? I need to get my baby. Go find your baby.* Is all that kept racing through my mind.

My cell phone rang over and over. My desk phone rang over and over. I was trying to compose myself because I needed to go get my baby from wherever she was. What happened? Did someone hurt him? Did they hurt my baby?

I answered the phone. I don't remember who was on the other end, but it was a clone of the barber, weeping, which made me instantly more upset. I couldn't get the words out.

"What happened to Lionel!?" Was all I could say in between sobs.

"He committed suicide. He shot himself." The person on the other end said.

I couldn't breathe. It felt like someone had kicked me in the chest. The word suicide stabbed me like a butcher knife. *Lionel, killed himself? I just saw him! Where's I'yanna!?*

Only God was keeping me functioning. My thoughts raced and processed everything quickly and the worst-case scenario haunted me. Something in my gut told me I'yanna was not well. Lionel had been spiraling these past few days. I knew immediately I was living a total nightmare. I had to go find my baby. I had to go get her. He'd left her alone.

My keys. I have to go. Now!

I tried to collect my purse in a clumsy disarray and one of my co-workers who had stepped away to call her friends at the Clarksville Police Department began to approach me. She told me not to drive and that she'd found out some information about what happened.

My boss told me I should sit down. Some co-workers didn't know what to do and I could see them visibly shaken by everything that was transpiring. Customers had respectfully left and the office temporarily closed.

This was so bad. I knew whatever she was about to say was going to be so bad. Everyone's face was pale and stricken with distress.

I knew it. I knew it. I knew it.

I looked into my co-worker's tear-filled eyes. The co-worker sat down in front of me and I was crying before she spoke, puddles of tears just falling down my face. I couldn't bear her news. I knew what she was about to say was so bad as our eyes met, mother-to-mother.

I didn't want to hear it. I just needed to go get my baby.

"Fairlen, they found I'yanna in the house under a pillow," she said, her face crumbling with emotion. "He shot her," she said in a gentle quiet voice, as if saying it more gently would soften the blow.

I heard what she said and immediately weakened and started screaming. I don't remember hearing it and I was no longer in control of my emotions, my body, my mind.

The room went black for me. Everything was a blur. I was begging God in my head to help me. To wake me up from this nightmare. This wasn't real and it wasn't happening. I was shaking my head and had fallen to the floor.

My words were inaudible to me. The sounds coming out of me foreign. I could see myself distraught and inconsolable. My heart had literally shattered.

"He killed my baby," I sobbed, repeating the words over and over trying to make it make sense, trying to change the definitions and words, trying to undo the reality.

This was a mistake. Someone got the information wrong. A strong sense of denial hit me, because it couldn't be true. I had to get to his house, a hospital or something. She wasn't dead. This was a rumor. Someone got it wrong. I could get to her and figure this out.

As I got up and tried to grab my keys, one of my co-workers grabbed my arm and sadly nodded towards the door.

Two police cruisers had pulled up to the front of the business. Their blue lights were on. My heart dropped. It was true.

Two officers exited and were walking towards the building in slow-motion it seemed. I didn't want to hear it and I knew they were coming to give an official notification of kin.

I shook my head and the words, "No, God," repeated in my head as my internal organs felt like they were squeezing me to death. My face was red, swollen and streaked with tears. I couldn't breathe. My head hurt. The pressure was intensifying.

A police officer dressed in navy blue and one dressed in a white uniform came up to our counter and asked to speak to me.

My boss, Kristie, took my hand and assured me she'd be right there with me. She led me back to the conference room for privacy and the police officers followed. My other two co-workers also followed and with a hand on each shoulder and my boss holding my hands, we all were quiet as the officers began to talk.

These women, though we may have had our differences, we're godsends, because in this moment they physically held me up and were my stand-in family. I was grateful for their presence in the worst moments of my life.

The officers' voices were heavy and somber as they introduced themselves and removed their police caps.

"Ma'am we are so sorry to inform you that your daughter, I'yanna Rawlins, was shot and killed by her father, Lionel Montgomery who then committed suicide. We are so sorry for your loss."

They spoke the words professionally, but carefully and with so much emotion and regret. It was official.

Chills covered my arms and although I'd known, hearing them officially say it made it real. Each word had cut my heart open and it bled profusely and gave sound through my mouth as I wailed and cried, a sound that I'd never known. The mom in me shattered into a million pieces. A part of me literally died the moment I knew my daughter no longer existed.

It's weird, I still felt I needed to "fix it" somehow. I needed to figure out a plan, an organized plan to handle this. I needed answers.

"Where did he shoot her?" I asked, as I fought to gain my composure.

I felt the gazes go around the room as if they wanted to protect me from this detail.

"I just need to know," I said. "Why would he do this to her!?"

The officers explained they'd found Iyanna under a pillow, and it appeared Lionel had covered her with a pillow before shooting her in the head.

"He shot my baby in her head!?" How horrifying, offensive, disgusting and the most grotesque thing I'd heard in my entire life.

The police said Lionel then called a family member and told them what he did before taking his own life, the officer said.

I shook my head in numb disbelief. I gathered myself for a minute taking tissues and wiping my eyes. I thanked the officers and made brief eye contact. Their eyes were deeply grieved. They saw and knew how bad this was. They'd seen my baby dead and I knew by their sorrow.

The first officer shook my hand, held it and apologized for my loss again with such a look of compassion.

After they left, I felt extremely numb and in total shock. I didn't know what to do. It was a blur. I remembered when a family member died there were certain things we did. We called everyone. We figured out the funeral home, made arrangements, and wrote an obituary. We bought black dresses and nice shoes for the funeral. We gathered.

This was different. There were no written rules in losing your child. I felt charred and open like a fresh burn, raw, seared and in agonizing pain with no relief in sight. There was not anything to tell me how to organize my thoughts after losing my infant daughter to a murder-suicide. It truly felt surreal like I was watching myself in a horror movie.

There was a stillness and quietness in the air. My life had come to a complete halt, but the world was still turning. Time was still ticking and life still moving. But for me everything in me was struggling to keep existing beyond what was occurring in each second I took another breath. I needed to call Momma, my sisters. I needed my family.

Getting the words out to my mom and sisters was gut-wrenching. Each time I said it, it made it more real to me and hearing their grief shattered me repeatedly.

The screams and weeping were indescribable. The surrealness of it all was so enormous coupled with immediate denial, questions, pure emotional chaos, and sorrow that came with each call.

"I'm on my way, Fairlen, I'm on my way," Momma said through tears. "I'll be right there, baby."

News had spread incredibly fast, and my phone was lighting up with text messages, and had continued to ring every few minutes.

I retreated to the restroom to escape. My co-workers were on my heels taking care of me like a true family. I assured them I was OK, a statement that's never been a bigger lie. I had to think.

Think. Think. What to do next. Where to go. I was lost. I was in the dark.

I retreated to the bathroom stall, covered my face and prayed to God, in long gasps and intense weeping. I let go and lost it completely. It was a safe, private place, and I knew I had to gather myself and face my reality.

I asked God to save me and help me. I just prayed so hard my words were coming out loud but not making sense to me. I just needed God to lift and carry me through what felt like a mirage of my actuality.

My baby was dead.

My baby was dead.

I was shaking all over from sobbing so hard and then I abruptly took a few deep breaths and stopped shaking. Like a blanket, the peace of God covered me, and I switched on the autopilot of emotions and survival that would carry me the next one billion steps in my life.

The rest of the day was a blur. I don't remember how I got home. I don't remember who I spoke to. I just remember being at the hospital and making a positive identification of I'yanna through a photo. I remember just wanting my mom and her showing up at my house that evening. I collapsed in her arms and screamed and wept.

She'd recently left Tennessee after helping me get back on my feet and away from Lionel and just like always she was instantly there by my side. I never saw Momma fold, no matter how bad it got. I've never ever felt like I was in any place in life that I had to give up because of the strength of my mom. It was never an option. Even though I never had my dad, I knew my mom would be there. Even now, at 41 years old, I know my mom is going to find a way.

On the worst day of my life, my mom found her way to me fast. We cried in each other's arms. She stroked my hair and reassured me she was there. She had always had a way of easing my pain.

This time she couldn't. No matter what she said, *this* was still the hardest and worst day of my entire existence, and nothing could change the fact that my baby had been murdered and I'd never hold her in my arms again.

I lay in my mother's arms and we cried together for hours.

Chapter 18

Headlines

The shock of the murder-suicide involving the prestigious Montgomery's of Foster Funeral Home shook the city and surrounding areas. It hit the newspaper, radio, TV stations and social media. Everyone was talking about this unthinkable act.

I was living it in real time.

There were no other words but horrific and tragic to describe the loss of my daughter's life. I was grieving so heavily, and I realized quickly that I wasn't going to be afforded the luxury to compose myself and do it in private.

I'yanna's murder was huge news and rightly so, because it was such a disgusting and egregious act. She was only seven months old and the youngest homicide victim the city had reported in decades.

My tragedy was televised, live and in living color, and I couldn't hide for a second from the violent, horrifying reality of my baby's murder.

The day after I'yanna's murder, the local newspaper, *The Leaf-Chronicle*'s front page featured a big headline about the murder-suicide and a story about the crime scene. The sensationalized large headline sold the news that day, but no one told I'yanna's story.

Everything I read or saw created a sense of rage within me.

I'yanna was innocent, beautiful, and smart with such a bright future ahead and she was murdered by the man who was supposed to protect her. Yet, somehow in every article his family was speaking of him in such a great light. No one was speaking on behalf of I'yanna and no one had asked me anything as the true victim in this evil unimaginable act.

Why were they praising Lionel as a person in the media? Why were they pretending and supporting the family of a murderer? Why were they pretending like Lionel didn't have any issues?

Everything was slanted and polished in the media and heavy damage control was happening. While I maybe shouldn't have cared what was being said, it was my life being talked about, my child, my tragedy but no one had heard my voice or honored my baby.

I didn't sleep. I couldn't sleep. I was in momma bear mode and was ready to fight whoever and take some control of my baby's legacy.

It was like trying to control a tornado as the whirlwind of media and daily events of violent crime spun out of control. It did its damage and then moved on leaving destruction and despair in its path. This was an anomaly for me to feel this lost, empty, and confused.

The Montgomery Family commented in the newspaper about their loss. They said there had been no signs and Lionel seemed fine and nobody detected anything.

Nobody approached me or asked how I felt about my loss. To add insult to injury, the follow up story had a photo of my mugshot and the drama of my arrest, and our custody struggle was laid out for the community to make biased conclusions based on incorrect information.

Around this time, it was popular for media outlets to publish news on Facebook and the comment sections to be filled with keyboard warriors voicing their blind opinions. I tried to stay away from that battle because I knew it was in vain to try and fight public opinion.

However, I wasn't going to let anyone or anything paint false narratives of my tragedy. While my self-guilt had quickly begun the blame game in my heart, I wasn't going to allow strangers to further hurt me or my family.

The Montgomery Family were community figures and it seemed already they'd painted the picture of a solid but depressed dad desperate to have custody of his daughter and facing a vindictive, violent baby momma.

The article made me shake my head in disbelief. It was highly sensationalized. I don't believe anything the media says. There were very few accurate things in that article. It was very skewed and read like a tabloid not a tragedy. **Reading it just compounded my grief and added so much insult to injury.**

Father: Son was in court for custody issues before murder-suicide.

Lionel Montgomery Jr. had gone to court Friday with the mother of his child, Fairlen Rawlins, in reference to child custody issues before police say he shot and killed his 7-month-old daughter and then himself, said his father, Lionel Montgomery, Sr.

"(Rawlins) did have full custody (of Iyanna **Rawlins**)*," Montgomery, Sr. said, adding that "they went to court (Friday)" and were supposed to go again on December 26th.*

Montgomery, Sr. said there was no indication anything was wrong Friday before the incident happened.

"He came by and checked on me — I've been under the weather — so he checked on me and called his brother and best friend and they didn't detect anything," Montgomery, Sr. said. "He was in good spirits. I don't know what transpired (later)."

It was clear that politics played a huge part in how the story of what happened to I'yanna was being portrayed.

Everyone seemed to cater to the family with money, power and prestige. There was a disconnect between what Lionel did to my daughter and the response from his family and the community.

There seemed to be an agenda to create this honorable, respectable image of Lionel, despite what he did. It was like they didn't want to tarnish the great Montgomery name, so painting him as a psychotic murderer was out of the question. He got to be a troubled soul and poster child for mental health issues while my baby was mentioned like a small casualty of his internal war.

I was just a single mom, an ex-girlfriend of this man who seemed to have driven him to despair somehow. It was sickening, disgusting to me because no one knew the full story and the truth about who Lionel truly was beneath his shiny name and image.

As the days went by more articles came out. The more they came out, the angrier I got.

I voiced these concerns to my uncle who called the newspaper editor. My uncle gave the editor a piece of his mind about the pain being caused with these one-sided articles, mentioning arrests with no context, and showing favoritism to the Montgomery Family. He threatened to sue them for slander and a retraction was written, because so much information had been put out.

Soon a reporter was interviewing me, and I was able to share a few things about I'yanna. It was hard doing the interview but I had to be my baby's voice, so I did it.

It was very hard reading about my tragedy, but I told the truth about Lionel and cleared up some misconceptions.

Family recalls activity before killing, suicide.

Lionel Montgomery Jr. had gone to court Friday morning with former girlfriend, Fairlen Rawlins, for child custody issues before police say he shot and killed his 7-month-old daughter and then himself, said his father, Lionel Montgomery, Sr.

Rawlins said she had full custody of the child, I'yanna Rawlins, who lived with her.

"He had her on every other weekend," Rawlins said. Rawlins said she dropped her daughter off at Montgomery Jr.'s house around 11 a.m. Friday, just two hours before the shooting was reported.

Rawlins said: "It was no different than any other time."

Montgomery Jr. had "threatened suicide a few weeks ago, but the family didn't see the need for him to get help," Rawlins said.

"There was never indication that he would ever hurt our daughter."

Lionel Montgomery Sr., owner of Foster Funeral Home, said "he never said anything about suicide. He never brought it to my attention that there was trouble, so I didn't take it any further.

"If he talked to me about it, then I would have taken necessary actions to make sure he wouldn't do anything like that," Montgomery, Sr. said.

When Montgomery Jr. spoke with him before the shooting, Montgomery Sr. said everything seemed normal.

"He came by and checked on me — I've been under the weather — and he checked on me and called his brother and his best friend, and they didn't detect anything," Montgomery, Sr. said. "He was in good spirits. I don't know what transpired (afterward).

"Whatever it is, God will give us direction," Montgomery Sr. said. "I don't know what the problems were."

Remembering the Montgomery's, Rawlins said she wants her daughter to be remembered as a loving child.

"She loved everything around her and loved her brother," Rawlins said. "She didn't deserve to be murdered. We will miss her and always love her."

Montgomery, Sr. remembered his granddaughter as, simply, "beautiful."

As for his son, who served as Montgomery Sr. 's assistant at the funeral home, he said, "He was an all-around person, people loved him."

Montgomery, Sr. said the family is "doing fairly well under the circumstances."

Investigation.

There is no new information about the investigation, Clarksville Police Department spokeswoman Sgt. Cheryl Anderson said Saturday.

CPD Detective Tim Anderson, of the Major Crimes Unit, is lead investigator of the case.

Years later, I would read the official report by the lead detective. They destroyed all evidence of the case in 2009 although I'd asked to see the evidence and the crime scene tape. The detective told me it wouldn't help me and refused to show me. I never saw it.

The official police report said that Lionel left a handwritten note. It was simply my name and phone number which he then taped to his TV in his bedroom.

The note was the reason the police were able to contact me so quickly during their investigation.

Lionel did not leave a traditional suicide note explaining why he did what he did. It left so many unanswered questions for all the people left behind to grieve the loss of I'yanna and him. The shock and denial were overwhelming from those who just couldn't believe Lionel had done something so heinous. Experiencing such a public tragedy made me feel exposed and like I had no privacy. It truly felt like all eyes were on me at my worst moment and I didn't have permission to really grieve. It felt like everything was being watched and dissected. The vulnerability of it was tough to deal with and only with God and family was I able to cross each hurdle as it occurred.

The common question I got in those first few days was, "How are you holding up?"

Only God knows and only through his strength and power was I able to even function.

He directed my steps and kept me standing when I wanted to fall. I prayed by the minute, sometimes seconds, to keep breathing and not implode from sadness.

Those who knew me were in shock, searched for words of condolences and wrapped me in compassion. My family circled around me in support and love. I was always the strong one. The one who knew what to do.

Everyone was looking at me still in those moments and I often didn't have the words or answers to soothe their grief as I was the one going through the trial.

When I lost I'yanna, who I was as a person changed forever and it would take years for me to pick up my millions of shattered pieces to create a new sense of self through God's healing.

Chapter 19

Iyanna's Funeral

The reflection in the mirror looked foreign to me, as I applied foundation to my light brown skin. My home was quiet and only my thoughts filled the space. I looked at the woman in the mirror. She looked exhausted. Like life had suddenly aged her in a matter of days. Like something was missing from her.

But it was me, Fairlen. My eyes stared back, hollow from grief. A piece of my heart had been obliterated and a portion of my soul had been stolen. I felt I would never really be me again. I stared in the mirror, working to conceal the heavy puffy bags beneath my eyes.

Sleep had evaded me for days. Grief had beaten me mercilessly. I napped, waking up in panic from nightmares. Family had flooded my home in North Clarksville, as the news circulated. Now, I could faintly hear those familiar voices outside my bathroom door. They were mildly stirring about my home, being always careful and aware of me. I felt like I was moving in slow motion, my heart was so heavy.

The soul shattering cries I'd let out the past few days resonated in my body, but barrenness followed, and I felt void of tears. A soft numbness had set it, an uncomfortable stillness within me. It was the peace I'd begged God for and brought me unfamiliar moments of serenity.

Dread hung over me like a dangling anvil and I feared the fall.

I dusted my lids with eyeshadow, my lashes with waterproof mascara. I was trying my best to look presentable and knew all eyes would be on the grieving mother today. I'd been raised to always look my best even when I felt my worst. That was an Anna Hall lesson.

I searched my presence for the old Fairlen. I needed her to come out and be the strong, confident, woman who always seemed to have it all put together. I was a natural born leader. I loved walking in a room and working the room, making friends and connections. I was a businesswoman, a hard worker.

Today, I struggled to be me. I didn't even know her right now. There was no sign of order. Today was a day I felt like I was in another dimension, not of this present world. I wanted to hide.

'Fairlen, keep it together. Don't fall apart,' I whispered to myself, as I applied the smooth lipstick across my lips. It was the pep talk I'd been giving myself over and over. I couldn't lose my mind. I couldn't have a nervous breakdown even though I felt I was holding on by a thread. I still felt I had to wear a strong face for some reason, although I knew it'd be perfectly fine and expected to just lose my crap in these moments. But I was the strong one. I had to be, especially for family and friends.

I wished I could let it all out in that bathroom mirror, while I was alone. To just do it while no one was watching. But I was calm. I'd cried out all my tears before getting out of bed that morning.

The morning of my daughter's funeral.

I laid in my bed for almost an hour in the darkness. I didn't look at the clock. I didn't even want to be aware of time. I didn't want to anticipate the minutes and hours that I'd never forget.

I was awake, exhausted, but too anxious to close my eyes for another minute. Tears poured out my face. I buried my face in my cotton comforter. My body shook from my sobs. I didn't want to wake anyone in the house, but I literally felt my heart ripping. A broken heart was an understatement. I felt it opening, leaking, and pouring out. With each breath it split more.

I couldn't do this. I could not bury my baby today.

My face reddened as I still fought to hold back. But my mind emptied itself in the form of tears. And with a deep breath, I'd again go numb and stop crying.

For just a second, I slipped into a happy place just hoping for one more morning with her. It quieted my sorrow and at the same time sent me into a spiraling feeling of regret. Our mornings were always so rushed. I had to get her and her brother ready for the day. AJ had to get to pre-school and

I'yanna off to daycare. Then I had to rush to work by 8:30. Each morning I cleaned because God knows I could not leave the house in a mess because it just wasn't in my nature.

I regretted not slowing down to enjoy her more. I was always on the go. It was just me with my two children and failure was not an option, so I pushed hard to be sure that I could do it all on my own.

I just wished I could've taken in her little smiling face more. Squeezed her little chubby body for a minute longer each morning and enjoyed each second of her big gum exposing smile. I wish I would've listened to her coos and her "talk" more intently and taken in those very few milestones she reached before she was taken from me.

I could see her chunky legs fastly scooting across the floor as she learned to crawl. And she had a little of my independence and stubbornness as she used to snatch her baby spoon out of my hands to feed herself. Ooh, wee she'd make a mess eating because 'Yanna loved to eat. My little chunky, happy baby.

I just wished and hoped and imagined one more morning. I smiled as I thought about our last morning together and I cried knowing we'd had that extra hour or two to be together before she was taken away from me forever.

There would never be another moment of holding her, comforting her, watching her grow.

She was gone.

The thought sent me into breathtaking sobs again. Grief is the scariest of rollercoasters, abrupt, death drops, twists and turns and no matter how much you scream it never slows down.

How did this happen? Why did this happen? Please wake me up from this horrific nightmare. I was woke. *It* was real.

To say *it* out loud, think *it*, acknowledge *it*, this new truth in my life was repulsive and unbearable.

I knew things with Lionel and I had grown to a really bad place, but I never in a million years thought he was capable of such a foul act. This man who I'd at one time trusted, loved, and depended on, self-destructed like a helium bomb and obliterated everyone and everything he loved in a matter of seconds.

He took her from me, and he did it to destroy me.

I hate walking in unknown situations. I like to plan ahead and organize. This was so unfamiliar to me. It was something that was completely out of my hands. I had no control over what happened. In the aftermath, it scared me in many ways.

In a fit of hurt and despair that morning, I'd almost yelled to God, "I can't do this! This is too much for me! I need help."

He sent help. He sent strength. He sent me peace that day, as I reflect. He sent me calm as I prepared to do the hardest thing I'd ever have to do in my life.

He sent me solace the night before as I saw I'yanna deceased body for the first time. The process of burying someone you love comes in so many facets. That Monday, my mom and I went to the funeral home to make sure I'yanna was prepared for her service and that we approved of how she would be presented. It was one of the few things I had a say in during the process of her funeral and burial.

We pulled up to Foster's Funeral Home that Monday night. The light above the green awning was on and the white and green house perched atop the funeral home had lights on, too.

Lionel's family owned the funeral home and lived in the home above. I'd been there many times, but the amount of dread I felt this night was unlike any dread I'd ever experienced. I didn't want to stay long. I made it clear to Momma in the car and she reassured me we didn't have to.

Momma held my hand as we walked to the building and into the lobby of the funeral home. This was the traditional community funeral home, etched in pride, history, and generations of trust and respect. Lionel had prided himself in being a part of such a rich family legacy. He'd grown up in this home and learned the craft of his father. Families gathered here to lay their loved ones to rest. It had been the house of mourning for thousands in the community.

Tonight, it was our house of mourning - his family and mine. The irony of the mourning always being for everyone else, made this public and horrific tragedy feel extremely foreign to suddenly be so exclusive to just us.

The moment I stepped into the dank, dark funeral home that evening, my heart stopped cold. I felt like I'd stopped breathing. Things became blurry and I was just moving through space. My anxiety was soaring.

It was the first time I would physically see her since she died. I'd been allowed to identify her through a photo at the hospital, but this was the first time I had to lay my eyes on her.

Everyone spoke in hushed voices. Mr. Montgomery, the funeral director, was I'yanna's grandfather. He loved her and this hurt was too deep.

There was too much sorrow for eye contact. It seemed like a silence came over everyone, hearts were too heavy for greetings and salutations. It was just things that had to be done, processes that had to be completed.

Mr. Montgomery sauntered through the halls of the funeral home with us in tow and ushered us to a viewing room.

Although this was his granddaughter, it seemed he'd put on his funeral director hat and taken his emotions out of it. Like a funeral director does, he opened the door to the viewing room where I'yanna lay and left me and Momma alone.

Although we may not have seen eye to eye, I felt his pain in that moment of having to show me what his son had done to my perfect baby. How he'd tried to piece it all back together in his best attempt at restoring her dignity. I'yanna was his first grandbaby and he was supposed to watch her grow up, but instead he'd loved her for seven short months, and then he received and prepared her small body for eternal rest. I pictured this proud man weeping over her as he embalmed her small body, but at this moment he left us to continue the process.

Everything in the room seemed dark, except I'yanna.

She wasn't in a casket.

Instead, her small body was laid on a cold silver slab. Like something in a cold research lab. It seemed so unfair to me. A florescent light shined on her and illuminated her fifteen-pound body. She was still and looked heavy.

It was so hurtful. I couldn't really comprehend it.

She had on the clothes I'd chosen, but I almost didn't notice.

A beautiful white dress.

I couldn't gaze upon her for long. I just looked quickly. I felt I was standing 100 feet away, just gazing from afar, but I had edged closer.

She was beautiful and at the same time seeing her ran my blood cold and produced a horrific feeling of panic.

I didn't touch her. She looked like a sleeping baby doll. She looked presentable for her funeral.

Momma and I exchanged looks and may have said, "She looks … OK. Pretty."

But how do you describe a dead baby?

The grief and trauma we felt shook the other's emotions. We looked away and back at I'yanna for a second. It was time to go.

It felt like such a cold and mechanical process, but I did it.

I didn't want to dwell on it or process it at that point, so we looked, and mom and I were in and out in five minutes.

I felt uncomfortable trusting his family with the arrangements. They had taken a life insurance policy out on I'yanna unbeknownst to me, so not only could they afford her final costs, but would profit from the loss.

Despite my discomfort, I briefly thought of the Montgomery Family. Ironically, we shared something that was each our own... grief.

They'd have to close their eyes that night knowing their granddaughter and his son's dead bodies were in keeping below. It was a horrible thought and although we didn't agree on many things, including what led to this, I could relate to them on the sick feeling of utter devastation that rested in the pits of our stomachs.

The cool winter air stung at the hot tears rolling out of my eyes as I exited the building. Momma was holding my hand.

There were no words.

It didn't even hit me what I'd seen or even that she was really gone. I couldn't grasp it and I did not want to try to.

We drove off to face the next day.

And here it was ... the next day and the reality was entrenched ever more.

I felt safe being vulnerable by myself in my bed, but the strength, determination, and slight stubbornness I get from my Momma pushed through as I rolled out of bed that dark morning.

I had to get my son dressed. I had to get myself dressed and take time to gather my thoughts and composure.

Despite the strength from God, my human emotions and the unknowns left me feeling nauseous.

Despite me, there was AJ, my 4-year-old son. How would he handle this? He loved and adored his baby sister. They were extremely close. Since the day I brought her home, he was her big brother and took so much pride in that title. We were our own little family. What would he say when he saw her in the casket today?

AJ didn't understand death, and this was a big loss to try and explain it to him. How do I say, she's gone forever?

Would my family be able to keep it together? Honestly, I love them, but they've been known to wail and try to throw themselves in a casket at past funerals. I needed them to make sure I'yanna had a dignified funeral.

I put the finishing touches on my make-up, I stared at my mysterious reflection. I talked to God. Now it was time to stand tall… somehow.

Everyone expected me to fall apart. It was only natural when a mother loses a child in such a tragic way, right? At moments, I didn't really understand how I hadn't had a complete mental breakdown. How was I not in a straitjacket, heavily medicated, and talking out my head in some white room of a mental institute?

I knew God was keeping me strong, firm, and literally walking me through these steps. That's the only reasonable explanation. Nothing else made sense to me.

Momma checked on me, as I dressed in the bathroom. She wanted to make sure I was OK.

"Fairlen, come in here and eat something. You need something on your stomach, baby," Momma said.

My stomach was unsettled and my appetite non-existent.

"I'm OK, Momma." I replied, trying to sound convincing. She didn't push it.

I put on my white skirt and suit jacket. I was adamant we would not wear black. The dress I chose for I'yanna was a beautiful satin white dress. I wanted my baby to have an honorable and peaceful memorial. I wanted her to be remembered in a positive light because she had brought such light and happiness to all of us. I would not let her name be marred by the tragic way she'd perished. She was my princess and I wanted her to look like a princess that day. I'd picked a beautiful rhinestone tiara to rest atop her curly hair.

It's the strangest thought to think of your baby deceased, her small body in a casket, and still having the desire to make her look pretty. It's a thought I'd never fathomed even having.

I wanted to think of her kindergarten pictures and how cute she'd look snaggletooth. I wanted to imagine her at prom in a beautiful dress. I wanted to think of her on her wedding day and with her own family one day, but those memories would never happen. Like a magic eraser, I couldn't even visualize it anymore.

All I could envision was the uncomfortable and morbid image of what I saw last night. Even then I wondered if she'd look fine in the casket, if that was the right dress, and if she'd still look innocent and precious despite the filthy crime that had been committed upon her.

The dress was a beautiful white dress with ruffles and lace. It was a dress I'd picked out for her to wear for her first Easter or Christmas. Those are the outfits and pictures I wanted to put pride in. This would be my final, and really only, time to pick out a special dress for her. It was the only tangible thing I could take pride in. The only thing I had slight control over in this whole miserable ordeal and I held onto it. I held it with great pride.

I wanted her to have a traditional, respectable interment, and a dignified funeral.

I looked presentable, I thought as I smoothed out my suit, adjusted my hair and left. Autopilot is how I describe how I got through the day. It was a mode of survival.

Momma was busying herself scrubbing my already clean kitchen counters again. The smell of Lysol filled the house. She always kept a clean house and ran a tight ship when it came to cleanliness as she raised me and my two sisters.

Today, she cleaned to burn off nervous energy.

Her voice traveled across the house as she went into 'mom mode', asking questions, making sure everyone ate, got dressed and put things in order. She'd prepared AJ's clothes and my clothes and laid them out that morning. She'd cooked breakfast.

I promise I felt she'd cleaned my house constantly since she'd arrived that Friday. I don't remember how my mom got to my house that Friday. While it was days ago, it felt like a far-off memory, a blur of actions and movements that told a silent story.

All I know is she was here.

Momma loved her grandchildren; she was very involved and called me multiple times a day to check on I'yanna and AJ. It was almost as if she had this mother's instinct that something bad was lurking. It was almost paranoia how she called and inquired how I was doing, especially in the past few weeks as things had escalated between Lionel and me.

She did not trust him much, so to ease her mind she would frequently check in to be sure we were all safe.

The months before had been turbulent, she had just left Tennessee three months prior. She had come to rescue me then. Lionel and I's relationship had hit the final straw. She had set me up in my own house and made sure I didn't have to rely on him.

Besides just being there during those hard first days, Momma helped me find my voice, especially as we made arrangements for I'yanna's funeral.

I decided to have the funeral as soon as we could, within the week, and urged everyone to arrive within days after the murder. I didn't want to prolong it. The only tradition I didn't want to stick to is waiting forever, the usual week or two, to bury her. I planned her service very fast to get it over with. The fact that everything was moving fast was a good thing for me, but the fact that there was so much happening in each second made it overwhelming and hard to digest.

Making her funeral arrangements presented a blatant truth to me. There was no love involved when it came to the other side of this tragedy. In fact, there was a divide and there was no doubt I'd always be reminded of how I was viewed by Lionel's family. The word blame surfaced each time. Since Lionel's family owned the funeral home, they provided free services for I'yanna's funeral. But in the planning process, it was made clear to me they had their own agenda. There was a plain wood casket that I knew they'd planned to put her in.

No. Just no.

I was in such a fragile state and the situation was so heavy. I knew they were grieving the loss of Lionel and I'yanna and here we were having to do business with a ton of unspoken emotions. That day we went to make funeral arrangements, Momma looked at me only the way she could and told me with her eyes to 'speak up!"

"What do *you* want?" She had asked me sternly and bluntly, in front of them.

I spoke up stating my demands to Lionel's family. I wanted a pink casket. They told me they were unsure if they could get one on such short notice, and if so, I would need to pay for the casket.

I was infuriated and my anger blazed. I'm not paying for anything and how dare they ask. I knew they had an insurance policy for my child, so I knew they had the money to fund everything and more. I never saw a dime. I told them with great anger that she was going to have what I wanted her to have. I did not care how much it cost or what they needed to do to get it, but that's what she was going to have. Needless to say she was buried as I wished in a small pink casket.

I'm forever grateful for Momma's presence and her urging me to speak up for my baby. It was so evident that I was surrounded by love.

On the day of the funeral, Momma was taking care of everyone like she always does. She was ironing my uncles' clothes, helping everyone with their needs, and just busying herself. The family arrived and waited for the black limos to pull up.

My home quickly filled up with family. Momma, and my sisters Gabrielle and Monica had been there since Friday, and like we always had done as our own family, we found comfort with each other. My aunts and uncles, my cousins, nieces and nephews all gathered at my small family house. I could hear Aunt Chris and Paulette, Uncle Jeffrey, Uncle Irvin, and his wife Aunt Mickey conversing with each other. Uncle Anthony and Aunt Trish, Uncle Michael, my Great Uncle Jesse, all the familiar voices brought comfort. The support was apparent from my eldest family member to the youngest.

They all appeared, coming into the dark space that was my home and bringing a glimpse of light with their presence.

The various emotions swirled through my house, as we prepared for the inevitable. I could hear the momentary cries and see my mom and aunts wiping their tears before I could see. They comforted each other outside of my eyeshot and spoke quietly about their emotions. In front of me, they wanted to be resilient, but I knew they were hurting, too.

At times, the house was just quiet and somber.

Then in true Hall Family fashion, there'd be a burst of laughter.

Great Uncle Jesse asked my mom to "press his trousers." We laughed.

Gabby looked at me, and just like when we were kids started laughing for no reason. "What!?" I said, and that only led to more laughter.

This was truly Gabby fashion, my baby sister.

My sisters and I had always been close as my mom raised us to be that way. I never knew that that bond would be needed so strongly in our adult years as we went through life's hardships.

This day when I was to bury my baby, Gabby stared at me looking crazy, until I laughed.

I look back on that with a smile.

Our bond helped me through those first few tough days. As the big sister, I'd always felt they needed me and I'd always be there, but it was clear I needed them.

Since the moment they arrived, my sisters held me up without a question or a word. They just did everything I needed, much different from when we were kids. They helped me find my voice when I'd been silenced.

They helped me with a task no mother wants to do and for them, the aunts, it was extremely heart-wrenching as they realized the first time, they'd' see I'yanna would be in her casket.

When Gabby and Monica in Kansas. They'd made plans to visit and to come meet I'yanna, but as life happens, families get busy and money is tight. We'd planned to meet up for the holidays, but none of it came quick enough. They'd only seen I'yanna in pictures.

They learned more about her as they helped me write her obituary and planned I'yanna's service that short weekend. Even in such a heavy, hurtful time, there were moments where we smiled and laughed despite the pain.

In just seven months of life, I'yanna had made such an impact. There was so much to say. I was adamant that I wanted people to know who she was. She was so sweet, calm and happy. I wanted people to always remember my baby.

I was reminded the day we finalized funeral plans together, that the bond that we had built over the years as sisters was what I was going to need. There's nothing like your sisters.

Time climbed and soon the limos from the funeral home were parked in front of my house to take us to the church.

It was time to go.

I busied myself, making sure AJ was ready and tended to him. I grabbed my Bible and my purse. Everything began to move very fast.

The day of I'yanna's funeral it was unseasonably warm for December and sunny. Although we felt darkness, God was shining on us. I was thankful it wasn't dreary or rainy to intensify the gravity of the day.

My family is a family that prays together in celebration and lamentation. It was almost without preparation and automatic that we began to gather in the front yard. We formed a circle like we did at family reunions, parties, and funerals and like always we held hands.

The energy of sadness seemed to pass through us as we stood in that moment trying not to catch eyes to avoid passing the tears. It was a prayer circle like none of us had ever stood in. Usually there was no question who would pray. I had always led the prayer. Soon I noticed, those sad eyes were looking up and all of them were looking at me. I looked back at my family. Their eyes were heavy with hurt and sorrow. No one knew what to say.

Like always I prayed for my family.

I closed my eyes, and I began to speak to God.

In the strongest voice I could muster up, I begged for what we needed. The voice that came out of my body was solid, although I felt weak in my heart. So many times, this strong voice has emerged from my body. People ask, "Where does it come from?" My only thought is that it's not by my own will that I can speak through pain. I knew God was giving me, us, strength beyond our understanding.

I supplicated God, begging for Him to strengthen me and my family. I don't recall every word, but I felt it and I remember feeling closer to God and a reassurance we would make it through.

After 'Amen,' I opened my eyes and those same eyes were gazing at me in amazement, some with tears welled up in their eyes.

The sunshine seemed to illuminate us at that moment.

I realized then that God was carrying me. All of a sudden that picture that was on my mom's wall throughout my childhood finally had meaning.

"Footprints in the Sand."

There was only one set of footprints in the sand because He was carrying me.

As I positioned myself next to my son in the limo and we left, I peered out the dark tinted windows and in that randomly timed, weird way only grief can, it hit me very hard. My baby was really gone.

The heaviness was present, but peace hugged and comforted me as the limo maneuvered through town to my church, Faith Mission Ministries. I held my son's hand. I knew this would be his process just as well as mine today and forever. Something about his innocence would be lost and it hurt my heart.

The doors to the limo opened and we all stepped out.

The church that I worshipped at felt like a strange place that I'd never been to, but it was home, and I was glad to be in the presence of my congregation and friends. They'd welcomed me with open arms to have I'yanna's funeral there, when Lionel's family church made it clear I would not be welcome. I was not offended, as I had no desire to be in presence where myself and my family would not be welcomed.

It's weird when tragedy strikes, the worse side of people show up and show out. I had a mission and I would not be distracted.

That unwelcoming feeling rushed me like a cool breeze when I looked to my left as I approached the church.

Lined along the outside wall of the church was Lionel's family, including his mother who had just recently reunited with her son after many years of separation. Knowing that back story and knowing where we were, it was agonizing seeing her. It was one of the first times I'd seen her. So many times, I'd seen Lionel in drunken fits, sob over the relationship he'd lost with his mother. She'd left when he was a child and it was an emotional scar that plagued him. It was strange that I'd empathized with him for several years, but at this moment, I empathized with her.

She stood at the front of the line. Immediately my heart identified with hers. Here we were, two mothers, walking through the darkest points of our lives. Our babies were gone. Although her baby had caused my pain, at that moment all I saw was her as a mother.

I wanted everyone to wear pink ribbons to commemorate I'yanna. I'd brought ribbons for my family and for the Montgomery Family. I wanted to be peaceful and I wanted to show forgiveness and love even if I wasn't quite there yet.

I've always been a lady and politeness were part of my upbringing, so I greeted the family, while they stared at me. I walked down the line and gave each of them a pink ribbon to put on. One by one, they took the ribbon in silence. It was not much to say and eye contact was brief if it even occurred.

The silence seemed to scream at me. No condolences. No hugs. Just a ribbon hand off.

Finally, I got to Lionel's cousin.

She angrily snatched the ribbon from my hand and replied, "I can get it myself!"

It became crystal clear to me, at that point, we were there in the same space, but we were not together. We were separated by this tragedy. We were on opposing sides and somehow they blamed me for his actions.

I didn't have the energy or desire to retaliate. I simply walked on. It was a day of dignity for my child, no matter what.

My heart pounded as I ascended the steps of the church and entered the doors. Each step was loud to me all of a sudden. Each moment felt bright and intensified as I could hear the music echoing out of the building. It rang in my ears louder and louder with each step I took. The vestibule seemed unusually long that day. Although I was surrounded by people, I felt I was walking alone so to speak.

The funeral directors began to line us up to enter the church. We had opted for a traditional funeral service. It was clear the Montgomery's wanted to be separated from my family as they stood back and waited.

The funeral directors swung the double doors to the chapel open. As soon as those doors opened, I could no longer hold it together. As soon as the smell of the chapel rushed my face and I saw the small pink casket staring at me from the end of the aisle, my knees grew weak.

The casket was the tiniest casket I'd ever laid eyes on. I had seen many adult-sized caskets in my life, but nothing prepared me to see this small pink casket that personified the innocence, time, and entire lifetime full of memories that had been stolen from I'yanna.

The reality that my baby was inside of that small pink casket shook me to my core. This was really happening. This was really my life right now in this moment. I couldn't breath as each step I took brought me closer to facing my baby for the final time.

My heartbeat quickened and the tears welled and fell out of my face without restraint.

I couldn't stop it. There was no composure to try to keep. There was no fight left to do so. All I could do was weep, groan, and wail as my heart shattered as my eyes fixated on her small pink casket.

It was like grief, in all his sneaky ugliness appeared at that very second and slapped me as hard as it could in my face. There was no retaliating, just total submission. I crumbled from the attack.

My uncles stepped in and held me up as I walked down the aisle. They would lend their hands to holding Momma and AJ as we took steps closer to I'yanna's casket, which was positioned in the middle of the church.

Although my biological dad was there, I had never had a relationship with my father. It was my uncles who held my sisters and I's hands during life's big moments. They were there during graduations and childbirths, and today, they were here for us. Somehow, they managed to console their wives and be with us. I needed them and they knew it.

A photo slideshow played on a mounted TV as the song "Jesus" echoed through the chapel. So many beautiful flowers engulfed her baby-sized casket.

Through tear-filled eyes I took in the scene in a confused state of anxiety and a morbid sense of, what only I describe as, eager dread. I needed to see her to make sure she was OK, in a sense. I know that sounds crazy, but as her mother, her protector, her caregiver, I felt an obligation to make sure I'yanna was OK.

This slow walk down the aisle was long and heart wrenching. Onlookers wept as the sorrow of both families was on display. It hurt so badly.

There was a line at I'yanna's casket. I was near the back of that line. I could hear my family, his family breaking down ahead of me, at the sight of I'yanna. Each time they broke, my heart shattered even more.

This was not the aisle I pictured walking down to see my daughter. I anticipated walking with I'yanna for her wedding. She'd be beautifully dressed in white, walking toward the love of her life.

Today, I'd see her dressed in white not able to ever experience love or live a full life. As the line shortened, I got small glimpses of her. As I came face to face with my baby, time stood still. It was dreamlike. It was all so unreal.

Nothing could have prepared me to see my child laying lifeless in that small pastel pink box. My beautiful, sweet gummy smiling I'yanna was still, cold, and silent.

Oddly, it felt completely different than the night before. While, I couldn't look at her for long the night before, all I could do was stare at her and wish for another minute. I took every part of her face into my memory. I studied her closed eyes and still puckered little lips, her chubby cheek frozen in time, her head full of curly black hair. I stared and gently caressed her face. I forced myself to process the moment no matter how hurtful it was, because I knew this was it.

Momma stood to my left and AJ to my right. We stood in front of I'yanna's casket truly viewing and spending our final moments with her.

My sweet, happy, baby who just days ago I was holding in my arms, who had reached her milestones and was crawling, and talking in that excited baby babble, laughing, and giving the best fat arm hugs and spitty kisses, lay there lifeless. Gone.

Immediately, I realized all of the dreams I had for her simply disappeared. This would be our last time together.

She was gently nestled in the pink satin lining of the casket, her little head resting on a white pillow. Her dark hair was gently laid down. Her tiara perched on her curls. Her eyes and mouth sealed shut.

The way her legs were positioned I could tell she was asleep when he shot her. I felt at peace knowing she didn't suffer from her injuries.

Her small face was swollen and the bullet mark under her left eye was very visible. It left a distinct blemish on her perfect face, despite the mortician's heavy application of wound wax and make-up.

I touched her hair. I wanted to hold her. I wanted to protect her. I didn't want to say goodbye. I quietly talked to her. It was just me and her. It was like no one else was there for a second.

AJ on his tiptoes quietly peered over the casket at his baby sister. I picked him up to see her and our little family held that moment together for the last time.

He didn't say much. He didn't fully comprehend what had happened. He thought she was asleep.

As we stood in front of his baby sister, his inquisitive little mind had one question.

"Mommy, why does she have that mark under her eye?"

"It's where the angels kissed her," I whispered to AJ.

He didn't ask any more questions, he just looked and I felt his innocence slipping away and his world forever changing from this unexplained trauma. Months later he realized she was never coming back.

I kissed I'yanna's face for the final time. Her once soft fat cheeks that I often snuggled on, felt cold and waxy. She felt like a plastic baby doll. I touched her soft hair for the last time.

I stood there for as long as time allowed. I spoke to her in my mind, telling her I loved her and trying to think of everything I wanted to ever say to her in her life. My mind felt jumbled.

This could not be it. I realized I'd said and did everything I could. I turned to give others their moment to pay respect. AJ and I retreated to the first pew closest to her casket on the right side of the church and sat down.

Everyone approached us kindly, gently, speaking in whispered tones and providing hugs and handshakes. I don't even remember faces. I politely accepted the condolences as people approached me.

"I'm sorry for your loss."

"Thank you.."

"She's in a better place."

"Thank you …"

"Time heals. God heals."

"Thank you …"

The words were well meaning, and I accepted each one with an empty sense of comfort, yet graciousness.

Moments in life you just live them- empty and full- and God gives you the strength to move to the next moment.

The hugs and condolences from family, friends and church members came in waves before the service. We went through the traditions of a typical Black family funeral. It was debilitating at times.

The funeral directors marched in rhythm down the aisle with great dignity and esteem. They approached her tiny pink casket and one of them stepped toward I'yanna and gently positioned her inside the box for a final time.

Tears streamed down their faces as they did their job, a job that was especially hard to do for their baby cousin. I'yanna was their family and these were people who saw I'yanna nearly every day. I'yanna spent many afternoons at the funeral home hanging with her dad and her grandad. The funeral home workers were close family and friends that knew I'yanna and had watched her grow during her short life.

I sympathized with the funeral director who had been a very close friend of Lionel. Through his professionalism, he tried to be stoic, but tears were streaming down his face.

Today all those in I'yanna's village were part of her funeral procession. Sobs and sniffles could be heard throughout the church, as it grew quiet in respect. The funeral director gently stepped forward and slowly, ever so slowly, closed the lid of I'yanna's small pink casket. It clicked and locked enclosing her in darkness with finality.

The emotion in the room heightened in that moment and the cries grew loud as the finality shook us all to the core. My face flushed and turned hot with tears as grief gripped and held me. It was never opened again.

The pastor who eulogized her was Harold Browning, Sr. I call him my Father Pastor, because he is a spiritual father to me. He was the perfect person to put words, encouragement, hope, and faith to such a sad day.

I remember him speaking about innocence during her funeral. All the words were comforting. Since Lionel's family was there it was tactful. He never mentioned how she died or anything about the murder. He uplifted us and helped us cherish I'yanna's memory. I felt satisfied as his words flowed over the crowd. It wasn't just my pain. It was all of our pain. It was the dignity I longed for.

After the eulogy, we had a song and praise.

My best friend at that time, Yunetta, rose and walked to the front of the room.

I'd asked her to minister one of her beautiful praise dances as a tribute. I knew this was hard for her, because Yunetta was an auntie to I'yanna. Her mom owned the daycare where I took I'yanna and many days when I went to pick her up, I'yanna would be in Yunetta's arms playing or asleep. Yunetta had a daughter and our daughters were supposed to grow up together. Yunetta had been by my side and I felt her pain in my heart as she prepared for her performance.

Tears streamed down her face as she stood statuesque in her beginning position. She wiped them and composed. herself and primed herself to give this dance her all. I found myself holding my breath for Yunetta just hoping she'd be OK.

She'd expressed that she wanted to do it for me as her final goodbye to her niece. Her white gloves were poised in the air and her flag at rest. She was dressed in pink and white at my request. She ministered and performed a beautiful inspirational dance to the song "I Need You Now."

As the intro began, Yunetta began to smoothly move in deliberate movements.

She danced what my soul was crying, as gospel singer Smokie Norful's voice filled the church.

Not another second or another minute. Not an hour or another day. But Lord I need you right away.

If I never needed you before. To show up and restore. All of the faith that I let slip. While I was yet searching the world for more. The truest friend I have indeed. You are my best friend I know in me. I stretch my hands to thee. Come rescue me. I need you right away.

Her limbs stretched, as the piano heightened in the song. Her dress flowed delicately with every graceful movement. The display of emotion in dance was breathtaking.

The agony of being alone. Fear of doing things on my own. The test and trials that come to make me strong. The feelings of guilt, hurt, shame and defeat. The waves of trials that beat upon me. But to know, Lord, that in you I've got victory.

I need you now, Lord. I need you now, oh. I need you right now, right now, right now. I need you now."

The words ripped at my heart, tears streamed down my cheeks without control as I watched my friend *dramatize* the song's deep lyrics. I felt I had lived the lyrics of the song and more than anything I needed God to help and heal me right now. There was no other way.

Her arms stretched to the sky. Her body moved elegantly across the front of the room. Her face etched in passion and despair. I felt her emotion. I raised my hands in praise.

At the song's conclusion, all were overcome by emotion. The room was filled with applause and quiet with thick emotion simultaneously.

I had seen God make a way before, but it was for others. This time it was me and to be honest as I sat in the chair staring at my baby's casket, I didn't know how he was going to do it.

I needed Him more now than ever.

Time continued to climb quickly. Tissues. Tears. Hugs. More condolences.

We had to make the long trek to the cemetery.

There's dread and relief on the day of a funeral. You move through the motions and you just want it to be over, yet the finality of it all dredges a deep mixture of emotions that leave you drained. When it's your child, it intensifies each second of the day.

As we tucked ourselves in the limo, preparing for the long drive to the cemetery there was a knock at my window.

I slowly rolled down the black tinted window and Lionel's best friend stood on the other side. I jumped out of the limo quickly to hug her. She was in shock as we all were. She hugged my neck and began to weep.

In between her sobs, she whispered, "I want you to know that I don't blame you for what he did."

The words stung me, sliced me like a knife. What did she mean "blame me for what he did?" I jerked away and without a word, hesitantly reentered the limo. In silence, my thoughts grew angry.

How could anyone blame me? He killed *my* baby. *He* committed suicide. This was to hurt *me*. How can anyone *blame* me.

The thoughts consumed me as I quietly mulled over it all. I know she meant well but it was evident to me that there were some who blamed me for everything that had happened, and it infuriated me.

"You alright, Fairlen?" Someone asked. I felt the anger pouring out of my face and quickly fixed my expression, reassuring them I was fine.

I didn't notice the cars pulling over to pay respect or the small conversations in the limo. It was like we were just there at the cemetery in an instant.

We buried I'yanna at Concord Cemetery in the Montgomery family plot.

When we arrived, her pink casket was already perched above the open ground.

It was like a movie. Staged. Not real.

But as I walked across the withered winter grass, past the graves of many, it felt more and more real.

Despite the moments of sunshine, the ground was cold and hard. The eerie feeling of leaving my baby here to be covered in dirt sent a chill through me.

I held my son's hand as we gathered under the green awning, walked across the green artificial grass, and sat in the few chairs draped in fabric.

Her small casket rested atop a small open burial vault. It loomed between silver fixtures that would lower it into the open grave beneath. I could see the dirt freshly carved out to hold her eternally. Hands were on my shoulders. I don't even know whose they were. Those hands handed me a rose. I clutched the rose tightly.

Father Browning spoke a few more words and we prayed. I closed my eyes so tight. It was silent. It felt so final. So wrong.

The urgency I felt at the funeral home the night before ran over me again. I had to make it quick and not prolong the inevitable. I placed a rose on her casket. Touched its polished pink lid one final time and turned away.

It felt like slow motion in a movie as AJ and I walked away. I could see myself. I slid on dark sunglasses, held my head high and escaped to the limo. There was nothing else left to say, do, feel. It was over.

My family slowly filtered to the limo after paying their final respect. I could see them through the window, touching her casket, crying, placing flowers on top and retreating to the limo.

I studied the empty, cold, void cemetery that was so full of so many stolen souls. I fought back tears with all my might, but they slipped out from behind my dark sunglasses.

The odd December sun shined as I left my baby in the ground and began my journey of grief, that dark relentless horrible beast called grief.

As the limos rolled away, I noticed the tractor equipment was stationed nearby I'yanna's grave, in a cold stark symbol that everything was inescapable at that point.

The grave keepers had begun preparation on the grave adjoining hers. That grave would be filled days later with Lionel's body.

It was another helpless situation.

I'd never planned to bury my child, and when she died, I had no idea where to bury her. I felt like that's where I had to do it because that's where Lionel's family-owned burial plots. My church did not have a cemetery and I didn't know how to shop for a burial spot for my daughter. Death was the Montgomery's business, so of course they had a solution. So, in that aspect, I let go and allowed her to be buried in their family plot.

It sickens me that she had to be buried next to her murderer.

It was all such a foreign, ugly, sordid concept.

I sighed deeply, as the black limo exited a place that would become a place that would exacerbate my grief for years to come.

Chapter 20

Anger & Loss

They say there are five stages of grief and loss: denial, anger, bargaining, depression, acceptance.

I was forced out of denial the day I saw my baby's cold body lying lifeless on a slab in Foster's Funeral Home, but I lived in anger, and I lived there for a very long time.

Two days after burying I'yanna, I decided to pay my final respects to Lionel. I attended his funeral with a friend. I knew although I came in and sat near the back, the whispers that I was there would be loud. While I openly welcomed his family to I'yanna's homegoing, I knew I was not openly welcome to his. It was hard being in the presence of his family, who seemed to shift blame to me.

While I struggled with the guilt of trusting him with I'yanna, I knew things between us would never justify what he did. I was not indicating in any way I would keep him from his child or stop him from being the best father he could be. There was nothing in the world I could've done to cause him to believe this sick act was the best solution. Yet somehow, fingers were pointing at me.

I resented the fact I was the one who lost so much, and it felt like everyone was talking about how I could've prevented it. It seemed nobody took responsibility for the years of causing or enabling his destructive behavior, not helping him seek therapy as a youth for abandonment and mental health issues, or teaching him how to actually love.

I'd viewed his lifeless body in his casket as it lay in front of the chapel at First Baptist Church. He was dressed in a suit as he often was. His usually smiling face was still, wrought with desperation. I stared at his hard hands. So much destruction they'd caused in a matter of seconds.

Folded in his stiff fingers was a silver necklace his father had placed like rosary beads. The necklace said, "Daddy's Girl." What an insult!

The level of delusion that went into covering how evil and callous of an act Lionel had committed was strong for his family it seemed. It was almost like they were emphasizing the bond he had with I'yanna, but if he loved her so much why did he put a gun to her head and pull the trigger? He was a murderer and a coward. Instead of standing up and being a man, a real father to I'yanna, he'd betrayed her in the worst way. I was angry for I'yanna, me and my family. I was even mad for his family. They'd been forced to say goodbye to him at just 30 years old and this state of denial they were still living in was insulting to my grief process.

As I'yanna's mom I'd been forced to see my baby, with all her love, life, and potential... dead. There was nothing worse than that reality and I didn't have the luxury to pretend there was a reason why that made sense.

I didn't care that Lionel was depressed or desperate. He was always looking for a way out, and this was by far such a cowardly exit. I knew he had done this as a way to let me know he would never let me have our child and she would not be raised without him. He ended their lives to prove a point. I questioned how I could've ever loved someone who would stoop so low to hurt me so badly.

How could he look at our precious baby in her face with her rosy, red cheeks, her big brown eyes, and her big smile and do that? That's right, he put a pillow over her face. My anger blazed as these thoughts consumed me. Why didn't he just take his own life if he didn't want to live? What kind of person murders a baby?

This was senseless violence. Both Lionel and I'yanna had so much more life to live, and why? Just why did it all come to this abrupt violent halt and devastation.

Anger was a constant visitor in my mind, and it was an unwelcome visitor that disturbed my peace.

I wasn't mad at God. I knew this was not his will and he had not caused this to happen. I was angry at the situation and all the people triggering my emotions everywhere I seemingly turned.

I found myself mad at a lot of people I encountered and dealt with. Around the time of I'yanna's death there was murder-suicide of a famous football player that made national headlines. In that case, the man who sold the killer the gun was formally charged. Lionel was a convicted felon and they learned someone in Nashville sold him that gun. Why wasn't the person who sold him that gun prosecuted?

Thoughts like these visited my mind. How could this have been stopped? Who was going to pay for my daughter's demise?

As I attended his funeral, not as a family member, I looked around the church at all the people grieving him. It made me mad.

I was angry that people were there to support him. My thought process was they were there to support him and thus they were supporting his actions. The pastor stood up and wasn't the officiant, but it was at his church. He said we didn't know what happened, that Lionel could've slipped on soap and the gun could've gone off. It could've happened that way. I was livid. How dare they downplay what happened! The inference was he didn't kill Iyanna and himself. I felt disregarded. I felt like in death they were treating him like they did in life. They were more concerned with the family's image and his image, and they would do anything to excuse his behavior at the expense of my daughter.

The mayor at the time, Joey Pepper, was in attendance at Lionel's funeral, as well as other government officials who were even acknowledged and there to support the family. Not one of these people had shown up to attend my daughter's funeral or support me.

My anger blazed in the fact that my daughter was his victim, but we were being ignored and victimized all over again. I felt like I had a scarlet letter on me, like people were staring at me like I had done something and like they treated me like all this was my fault. I'd never held a gun in my hand, but somehow, although I never pulled the trigger, I pulled the trigger. I felt judged. It didn't make sense and people made up stuff to make it make sense and it was at my expense.

It took me back to the little girl who didn't have a daddy. I felt exposed and no one was there to cover me and speak up for me and talk for me. That was anger I had to process through. It was never with God, it was with people.

Lionel's casket was lowered in the ground next to I'yannah's freshly covered grave. I felt so helpless, because that's not where I'd wanted I'yanna to be buried, but his family had the land, the power and the money to call the shots. Then there was just me trying to hold it all together and fight all the quintessential elements of raw grief and hold the honor of my daughter's life above my own pain.

The anger and loss compounded with time at first.

I wasn't exempt from my own inner rage. Why did I trust this man? What red flag did I miss? I mulled over the day I'yanna was murdered and tried to think if I missed something he said or did.

But in retrospect, there was no way I could've predicted what was brewing in Lionel's mind, and that he'd self-destruct, and our daughter would be an innocent casualty in the war raging in his mind.

I had never had any inclination of violence and the rants and babbling he'd left on my voicemail were focused on him wanting me to feel sorry for him so that I would come back to the home we shared.

He'd never threatened to hurt Iyanna and had never even owned or carried a gun. We had a court date coming up for custody but had been amicable in our arrangement and he had successfully kept and cared for Iyanna on his weekend several times.

The last time I saw him, he was calm and gave no inclination about the heinous act he'd planned to carry out. My mindset not to deprive Iyanna of her father's love played a big role in our co-parenting, but what he did was the opposite of love. Pulling that trigger and ending her life was the ultimate betrayal a father could commit against his daughter.

I wasn't the only one who had to work through emotions. AJ was very affected by the death of his baby sister.

While he was very young when it occurred, he suffered from PTSD and would go on to be diagnosed with other issues that may not have been caused by his sister's death but were intensified as he worked through the complex emotions of loss and grief at a young age.

AJ was put in therapy after I'yanna's death and we figured out along the way what his needs were and how to meet him where he was.

AJ would act out a lot and get in trouble at school. The behavioral issues were linked to attention, whether it was negative or positive attention. It was embarrassing and hard. I had to pick him up from school many times for his behavior.

I just wanted him to act right and he couldn't. He was eventually diagnosed with ADHD, PTSD, and Oppositional Defiance Disorder. I didn't want him to be confined to medication. It took a lot of work to deconstruct but therapy and church helped him a lot.

As an adult, he's doing so much better. He went through some hard bumps, but he came out of it well. AJ loves his mom. He loves me beyond measure. He is that boy who's going to make someone a great husband. He is loving, giving and caring. He's truly sweet, loves me, and is concerned about my well-being. We have a beautiful relationship. I really love him for that, and AJ has been my greatest prayer and victory.

Chapter 21

The Quiet

After I'yanna's funeral everyone went back to their normal lives. Momma had taken time off work and was one of the last of my relatives to return home. Something about her leaving left me and AJ with the quiet, stark reality of what our life now was. A sense of emptiness lay heavy on me.

I missed my baby. I felt I was still in a state of disbelief and shock that so much had occurred so fast and my arms were now empty without my baby to hold, cuddle, kiss and love. Just the thought of her soft, fat cheeks, or even the smell of the pink Baby Magic lotion would create this painful crave in my heart to hold her. I'd sometimes spiral in thought reliving various memories that I wish weren't etched into my memory. Sometimes like flashes I'd see the bullet mark on her face, the necklace in his hands, her grave, the flowers.

Certain songs would bring me to tears, both secular and gospel. Just hearing the deep emotions, I felt displayed in lyrics was often overwhelming.

Some days I felt I was just existing and other days, I felt I was a step ahead of this relentless beast called grief.

Early on, I'd wake up every morning and realize, this is my life. I tried to pick up the pieces, but I just wanted to hide.

It felt very raw to experience such a public tragedy. I knew everyone had probably moved on, but for me it was still in the headlines and I felt watched and judged. Even something simple like going to the grocery store, I felt the stares and whispers, even if it was mostly in my imagination. I was the woman whose baby daddy murdered their daughter and then committed suicide. It was truly like I wore *The Scarlet Letter* in my head.

I knew for my sanity, I had to really start leaning deeper into my relationship with God. I prayed all day, just talking to God, asking for mercy, grace, and strength to beat this Goliath of a trial. I knew without God that this trial would take me out both spiritually, mentally and physically.

I started going to church more and it was a young baby in the congregation that led to me facing my fears and grief head-on.

A baby girl at the church was in need of clothes. I knew I had a plethora of baby clothes to give from I'yanna's closet, but I also knew I'd be giving away the few things I had left of I'yanna. When I'yanna was alive, I bought her so many clothes and cute outfits. So many of her clothes were still new with tags. She truly wanted for nothing. But all her belongings were still hung in her closet, in her room that I had not touched, or visited since her death.

I couldn't bring myself to go into her room that was still decorated in Precious Moments decor. The lights were off, and the door stayed closed.

I knew beyond that door were remnants of the things she owned during her short life. I knew I'd have to go in her room eventually, but I never knew how hard it would be to face my grief head-on. Being in there and knowing she would never be back tore my heart out.

The night I went into her room to collect a few items for the baby at the church, I found myself immediately overwhelmed and overcome with all the emotion. As soon as I opened the door and her sweet scent hit me before I could even turn the lights on. Everything I had felt just collapsed on me and I felt myself just crumple to the floor onto her soft white circular rug. I could not stop the tears and the screams.

I just wanted my baby back! I just needed her back so I could raise her and love her! She didn't deserve to die. She didn't deserve any of this and I just needed this nightmare to end.

I'd been so strong and so stoic at times throughout the funeral and burial, but it all fell on me at this moment. I'd always been taught to cry behind closed doors and do it quickly. But it was all so heavy, and I couldn't stop myself from sobbing as I lay collapsed on her floor. I felt I would never get up and I cried every tear I had out until my head pounded and my face was hot like it was on fire.

"I can't do this," I sobbed my face buried into her rug. I couldn't breathe. I felt so overwhelmingly broken.

I knew that I was at rock bottom. I lay on her white carpet for what seemed like an eternity.

It was in those moments I first heard the voice of God.

God speaks in various ways. It's a small voice. Some call it intuition, but it's the voice of God. There's times I could audibly hear His voice. It's the strong conviction and knowing. It's an intense feeling and conviction.

The voice of God was audible like a real conversation.

"Did you know what she needed when she cried?" The voice of God asked me.

"Yes." I answered in between sobs.

"You knew when she was hungry. You knew when she wanted to be held. Fairlen, I know your cry. Cry out to me. I know what you need," God's voice said to me. "I cannot fix what you don't tell me."

"You're going to have to fix it, God." I said.

It would be some time later that I realized the magnitude of what I'd asked God... to fix it. To fix me. To help me. To save me. Please.

But how do you fix the murder of your child? How do you fix a shattered heart?

I realized these horrific things had happened to me, but it was still something God could fix. I was someone God could fix.

I knew my journey through the murky waters of grief was not going to be easy, but that night as I let all my feelings show and slowly went through I'yanna's clothes and picked out a few things I felt a glimmer of hope.

I came to her christening dress in her closet and I asked God to please give me another daughter one day who could wear this dress to her christening. I felt God promise me he would.

I heard the voice of God say, "Save that for your daughter."

I didn't know when, where or how, but I knew one day I'd have another daughter.

A lot of quiet moments along the years and reflection helped me reach new realizations along this journey. Sometimes I'd hear it in church. Other times I'd be watching TV and have an epiphany, but God started helping me piece together my peace. It took more than a decade, and still continues to this day, as I learn more about myself and honor my daughter's life.

Guilt was an emotion I wore like a coat for a long time. I blamed myself for my daughter's death. I knew others blamed me, too. I was in defense mode, but a part of me also fought that emotion.

I dealt with so much guilt and regret. Why did I let this destructive man in my life? Why did I trust my mind and body with him? Why had I walked away from my marriage to Adrian and made all the choices that I felt had culminated into the destruction that ensued? What did I miss? Why did I trust him with her?

I did have to sit and reflect on these feelings, but I also had to learn to give grace and forgiveness, which was very hard. The facts were, I had been going down a bad trajectory in my life before I'yanna's death. I wasn't being led by anything spiritual in my life, but my own fleshly understanding and desires. Part of fixing me was realizing that my daughter's life was not in vain. In fact, I'yanna saved my life. Losing her disrupted the cycle I was in of toxic choices.

God released me from the guilt in time, but I had to own up to the part that I played in the situation. I didn't give him the gun or cause him to do any of what he did, but I had to realize my decisions played a part in the overall outcome.

Forgiveness developed in me by faith. Meaning I didn't really want to do it but I knew that I had to. I knew I had to forgive very early on.

The day after I'yanna was murdered, I laid in my bed crying my eyes out. I remember God saying to me that I would have to do it (forgive) before I could heal.

My response to God was, "I want to obey, but I need help." Early on I thought that the forgiveness would only be with Lionel, however the enemy began to give me so many thoughts about myself and how I was such a bad mother and so promiscuous. I soon realized that I had to forgive myself.

Then came what others were saying about me and blamed me for the incident, so I also had to forgive them. All the anger I had towards so many in town who I felt supported a murderer, I had to really pray about to turn into deep forgiveness. They didn't know all the details, and nobody really knew how to handle such a sad situation.

Like God had forgiven me and shown me mercy and grace, I had to take time and to process my emotions and then truly do the same to others. It freed me. I had to learn to trust God and forgive in order to heal. There was no way around it.

Now forgiving others was one thing, but there was one person that took me the longest to forgive, and that was me. Forgiving myself was so hard, because I'm human and the what-ifs ate me up for a long time. However, when I look at who I was at that time in my life, I had to see that I was a woman broken-hearted and let down by disappointments in life. I was very lost in a way and really doing what I thought was best for myself and my children at the time.

Not all decisions were based on wisdom, discernment, and truth. I wasn't being led by a spiritual head or Holy Spirit. I was just walking. The men I chose were indicative of the lack of love from a father I'd had. It wasn't until I allowed myself to experience the love of an earthly Father in the form of my pastor, Harold Browning, Sr. and the love of God, as my

Father and to see, feel, and experience unconditional love that I actually understood what it was and that changed a lot for me.

When someone hurts you, you want to see someone pay for the way they hurt you. Often in crimes, there's this process of court, victim statements and sentencing hearings, but I didn't get any of that. It was an open and shut case, closed by suicide. I didn't realize that the finality of it all wore on me. To add to the injury, there were so many negative things being said about me as a person and why this happened. It infuriated me that it was said I drove him to do this. That was far from true. Lionel had mental health issues and addiction problems, but he was dead and at times I wanted to know who would pay for my daughter's life?

One of the things that helped me. I heard a pastor preach, she ministered the scripture, "Vengeance is mine says the Lord." I had to speak over my life that God would be my vindicator and rely on the character of God. I had to believe that he would vindicate me and help me to let go of people's perspective of me and hold onto God's perspective of me.

I would hear such horrible rumors being said about why Lionel did what he did, like he caught me cheating, but in actuality he was the one cheating. We weren't married and nothing justified him killing my daughter.

The emotions were so big some days, so overwhelmingly heavy. Somedays multiple things attacked me. Things I thought I'd worked through would resurface, but God would always send me an answer to my prayers and helped me work through my emotions and feelings.

I know it sounds crazy, but I literally had to repeatedly say out loud, "I forgive by faith." It became my mantra as I worked through heavy emotions and as I started to rely more on my relationship with God. It became possible to do the impossible. Forgive.

It's been a walk of faith to learn forgiveness and a battle between the mind and heart.

My imagination and thought process would take me to the depths of my anguish as I processed everything in those earlier days. If I saw someone I knew in public and they didn't speak, my mind would take me straight to the negative thoughts that they didn't like me, were judging me, or blamed me for my baby's death. That would uproot all the feelings of anger and I'd feel so exposed and vulnerable.

I began to pray a lot and really devote myself to prayer. It was my trust in God that taught me how to release and forgive and it was a long and painful journey. I went to therapy after I'yanna's death, and my therapist asked me how I dealt with conflict and tribulations in my life.

She later define that when I had conflict with others, if I had been offended a switch would turn me off and there was no turning it back on. When I was done, I was done. I could turn all emotion off and walk right pass you like you didn't exist. She asked if I had ever been able to turn a switch back on once I turned it off. The answer woke me up. I had not. If I didn't learn to turn the switch back on in this situation and shed light on it, the darkness would eventually swallow me up.

It was then I learned I had been operating from a childhood trauma response. I felt, and still at times, the need to protect myself because I never had anyone to protect me. That's how I self-preserve. I am still a work in progress. I still have to deal with that and give that area of my life space to relieve quickly. If not, it sets up in my heart. It was and continues to be through prayer, counsel and therapy, and getting to know me that I battle the things that made forgiveness of the situation of losing I'yanna hard.

I say the situation, because in time I experienced a clarity that turned my initial disgust and anger towards Lionel into a more spiritual outlook of the entire situation. When I pondered over the entire situation, one thing was clear, Lionel was just a vessel for the Enemy to carry out his attack. People ask me how could I not still be mad at Lionel? This is when I always share with them the *ah ha* moment I had while watching an episode of the *First 48* some years later.

God gave me revelation on understanding the spirit that was in operation when Lionel did such a heinous, cold thing to our baby daughter. Lionel was just the body the Enemy utilized to carry out his plan. I had to really study and have a deeper understanding of the spiritual world to not be mad at Lionel.

This particular episode of *First 48*, was about an altercation between neighbors about lawns and property lines.

It got so bad the man stabbed and killed his next-door neighbor. When police interviewed the murderer, he was an upstanding citizen that had never even had a speeding ticket.

So how did he commit such a violent, vicious act that seemed so out of character? I remember being enthralled in the show and the man said to police that, "It was like something came over me and I blacked out. I don't even remember stabbing him." Once he'd stabbed the man, he said it felt like whatever had come over him, "lifted off him and left him."

That's when it all came together for me, and the Lord ministered to me. He shared that when you've given the Devil, or the Enemy, a place and you hadn't guarded your gate you can be ignorant. I believe that same spirit came upon Lionel and when he had done what he did to I'yanna he had no recourse but to take his life. The Enemy doesn't play fair and doesn't care. His job is to steal, kill and destroy. That's all he does.

The Enemy had me on his radar and he'd done all he'd needed to do to finish me off. I had to start studying more about the Enemy to really understand my spiritual journey that I was on.

When the Enemy was walking the Earth to and fro' seeking to devour, I had to remember that the Enemy never changes his job description. Every day, all day, 365, 24-hours, he's walking the Earth to and fro' seeking who to devour, and he doesn't care if it's a Christian, Atheist, Buddhist, or whoever. He doesn't care.

As believers, we change our job descriptions and we get distracted by life and because we aren't on our post spiritually we become the one who He can devour. Lionel was a willing vessel and I was a by-product. The Enemy doesn't care how he does what he does, he just needs to do it. The spirit in operation gave me peace because I had a greater understanding.

The Enemy is not looking to knock you off kilter. He's looking to destroy you. I understood at that moment the enemy wasn't trying to distract me or throw a monkey wrench in my plan. He was trying to kill me.

The best result for the Enemy is for you to be the walking dead. He doesn't care about you walking the Earth void, rendered with non-identity and no authority or power. He didn't care if I was broken with daddy issues, distraught about what happened to my daughter at the hands of her father. He didn't care about me breathing or living in prison. He cared about my effectiveness.

I had trouble understanding what the plan of the Enemy was, and once I understood his plan, I could counteract it. I could choose who I wanted to be and how I could do better. The Enemy has an agenda for your life and he works tirelessly learning to beat you at your own game. I decided I had to fight the Enemy and I knew to do that I had to become a part of the spiritual warfare I'd been pushed to the frontline in.

If I was going to keep my mind, I needed something solid to hold on to and God showed me very early, he was that solidity I needed to survive.

Later, I had to deal with condemnation within myself, the what-ifs, the "it's my fault that…" All drove me to a dark place and the enemy began to bombard me with condemnation.

I was thinking if I had not been in sin or if I'd been doing God's will I would've been able to see and discern the calamity in my present and future from being yoked with Lionel in that toxic relationship. It was a cycle. I had to deal with the condemnation of being out of position and being in sin, and dealing with the cost I had to pay, which was my daughter's life.

With spiritual clarity came understanding and that understanding helped me process and heal so many raw emotions.

All these things I speak of did not occur in a few days or months. It took years of me really working on myself, but there were things along the way that God did to elevate me to the next level of growth and healing.

One of those physical things was the presence of a family who had been there from the very start, even before I'yanna was born. It was many interactions with them that would change the very shape of my heart and allow me to experience the full reach of unconditional love.

Chapter 22

Harold's Heart

I hadn't been consistent with going to church. I'd be in and out of church sporadically. I knew I should go to church and had been raised in the church, but it wasn't practical when I was busy doing my own thing.

I'd pop in once a month or every other month at Faith Mission Ministries and had even had AJ dedicated there in 2003 when he was a baby. I'd been going irregularly since I'd moved to Clarksville and the First Lady Gwen later said she'd always notice when I was there. I wasn't an official member, but I was becoming a more permanent fixture after I'yanna's death.

They'd welcomed me when I'yanna died to have her funeral there and the pastor, Harold Browning Sr., a 5'4, chocolate-complexioned man, had spoken such beauty over my baby's life and in the process spoke life into me during my darkest hours.

On the day of I'yanna funeral, he embraced me, as he and his wife had done even before my tragedy. He told me, "Now, your ministry begins."

I didn't know what that meant at the time, but throughout my spiritual journey it's became clearer and clearer my purpose and my fight to both encourage, motivate and inspire a variety of people going through the toughest trials.

When I was at my lowest, Harold Sr. and Gwen, pulled me in with love and care and it was life-changing for me. They checked on me often and offered their support, not just in words but in deeds.

I felt such a closeness to them because they took an interest in AJ and I and have taken us under their wings since I'yanna's death. They really cared how we were doing. They would do simple things like, Pastor Browning picking AJ up to spend a day with him, taking AJ to get a haircut, not professional but a decent one, and they pastored me. At a time of great vulnerability, they were approachable. I was just a parishioner. It was them checking in on me. I was by myself and didn't have anyone else. They really loved us. It was nothing asked for, but they'd pour into us. I started to receive that love and support from the church and the congregation. I knew I needed something to hold on to and keep myself stable. I found that peace in prayer and worship with the Browning's at church.

During my spiritual journey, I realized something very crucial in my walk with God that had played a huge part in the way I moved as a young woman.

Because I did not have a father naturally, it distorted my view of my Heavenly Father. I couldn't fathom having a father who would love me and want the best for me. I couldn't perceive that because I'd been raised in the circumstances of a father who had forsaken me.

In the Earth realm I felt my father didn't love me, had broken promises, and I wasn't his priority. My sisters' father were involved, but as a child I wondered what it was about me that my father didn't love me or accept me. The broken relationship with my father distorted my view of God. How could the one I could see not love me, but the one I couldn't see love me?

Harold Browning, Sr., began to truly father me. It was the first time I felt like a man, an older man loved me like a father would. He saw past the flaws and saw my heart. Whenever I spoke with him and Gwen, I always left feeling higher, encouraged, and loved.

He really loved me, and God allowed him to see my heart. He encouraged me and spoke life into me every time he saw me.

From the time I met him, I knew he was always different. He was very different from what I thought a preacher was. Growing up I was a part of a Baptist church. I had always seen preachers that preached on Sundays but had a girlfriend outside of marriage on Monday. Pastor Browning was different. He really lived what he preached on Sundays. I was always afraid of him- not a bad fear- but I have great respect for him. He was the first person to tell me that God had called me to make an impact for the Kingdom. I would go to church and he would preach exactly what I was thinking.

Gwen and Harold, Sr. had three sons and as I got more acquainted with the various members of the church, one of their sons would unexpectedly bring love and more healing into my life.

I knew Harold, Jr. as the guy who played the drums at church. I didn't pay any attention to him. It wasn't like that. I was not looking for a man. In fact, when I met Harold, Jr. I was actually trying to reach his younger brother to inquire about coaching AJ's t-ball team. I'd become a part of the singles ministry and the coordinator for the ministry was telling me I needed to talk to Timmy Browning because he was a star baseball player and could really teach AJ baseball.

I kept trying to get in touch with Timmy but I could never get him. He was young and busy. As a substitute, my singles coordinator asked Harold, Jr. to help. At the time, Harold, Jr. was more settled, saved, and really involved in church.

The first time I called Harold, Jr., we talked for three hours straight. It was very naturally easy to talk to Harold, Jr. It was like instant friendship and it wasn't complicated.

Losing I'yanna was fresh, and he'd been watching me go through it from afar, but he spoke so openly and kindly to me about my emotions. I found myself really captivated by our conversations.

Harold Jr. was very different from any other man that I had ever spoken to. It was like I had known him all of my life. He made me laugh and that was something that I had found challenging in the months after my daughter's death.

He was a very intelligent man and spoke with such great wisdom. He was a shorter, chocolate man, and very attractive. He had a beautiful smile and the more I got to know him the more I noticed his qualities.

He became my calm in a world that seemed so untrustworthy. He was a friend at a time when I really needed someone. I remember his voice urging me to find solace in prayer and telling me that I was not a failure, and that no matter what my mistakes were that God loved me and would always love me. During that time of healing, I needed to hear those reminders so badly, and it was so reassuring.

Harold, Jr. always told me how good of a mother I was to AJ. He made sure that I knew that. I recall feeling like I had really failed at protecting my daughter and Harold, Jr. assuring me that I had done all that I could to be a great mom to them both.

I was so afraid to be vulnerable again because I really did not trust my decision making as it came to men, but he made it easy to open up to him. For the first time in my life, I was open to a man, and I told him everything about me. I was expecting him to walk away, but he stayed and held my hand through it all. Harold, Jr. became my hope that I could love again and be loved.

Unlike with relationships in the past, talking about our spiritual journey had no boundaries. There was no atheism lingering and there was no debauchery on the backburner with a side of church on Sunday like in relationships past. It was really freeing and faith-strengthening to pour out my heart and feelings about God and receive the gift of reciprocation and spiritual encouragement. He helped me to mature spiritually. He was there to help me even when I did not realize I needed help. He saw that I was a mess and he stepped up to the plate to help walk me through healing.

We truly had instant chemistry, and I experienced what it meant to be evenly yoked for the first time. It was such freedom and a sense of security knowing that this was a man willing to answer to God about me.

Where I was at in my mindset and heart it was almost scary to feel these feelings. How could I trust myself? How could I ever trust a man again?

Harold, Jr. worked at the Trane air conditioner factory, and I'd talk to him for hours through his shift. Despite us both trying to fight it, there was a connection and each time we hung up, it felt more like that romance that left you wanting to never stop talking. We were drawn to each other and would be hanging on to the last word. The more we talked the more we both knew there was something there, but we were both fighting internal battles between mind and heart.

Harold, Jr. said prior to me calling about t-ball, he had been praying for a wife and his mom had asked if he thought the Lord was preparing me to be his wife. He said no, because I had a child and he was very set on not having children.

However, he said it was in the back of his head and one day when he came into Bible study at church, he saw me sitting there in and as he passed me, the Lord said, "Enjoy the wife of your youth."

A few months later, at a family prayer before Wednesday Bible study, he saw AJ sitting in my lap and I was praying over my son and something in his heart changed in that moment.

We dated and got married on October 24, 2008. We didn't have a formal wedding. We got married in my father-in-law's office. He officiated the wedding. We didn't have money to have a big wedding. He was a pastor's son, we were ready to put our lives together and live together. So, we wed and had a reception a month later.

I'm a hopeless romantic. I've always believed in love. I didn't want to be by myself. I've always wanted to love and be loved. Even as I was healing from such heartache, I knew I wanted to love again. It was Harold, Jr. who would task me with digging deep, past the hopeless romantic to doing all the work it takes to have a successful marriage.

Harold, Jr. was on my journey with me as I healed from so many things and learned about marriage and how to be a wife. One of the first major fights we had was about AJ, and in retrospect all the pain and fear I had as a mother surfaced in that fight.

AJ had done something and Harold, Jr., who had developed a very close bond with AJ yelled at him and threatened to spank him. Everything I knew to be true about my husband went out the window and I snapped. I went into momma bear mode and all the emotions welled up. I wanted to protect AJ.

Although I knew Harold, Jr. loved my son and my son loved him, all the pain from losing a child to violence, the fear of my child being hurt just surfaced. I was yelling at him not to yell at my son and not to talk to him like that. I was always very particular about everything concerning AJ, but Harold, Jr. never treated him differently and treated him like his biological son from day one.

I knew I had more healing to do to trust a man. Everything I saw and been taught from infancy about men had to be healed if my marriage was going to be successful. We both had work to do with and for each other and the beauty was we were both in it and letting God lead the way.

Although I'd been married before, marrying Harold, Jr. was different. He wanted to be a spiritual leader. I'm an alpha female, and I constantly rearrange myself to respect the spiritual leadership of my husband. I've had to learn to be submissive. I still work to remember to look to him in things that I used to take the lead in. When we first got married, spending money, discipline, and making plans were all things I had not considered him in. It took me, and still takes me, to bend my will and desires, not to offend him or cause friction. It was difficult and took me being truly accountable.

Accountability holds you accountable for your foolishness. When someone calls you on your things, it takes a lot to be aware of them. Harold, Jr. and I had to understand our differences. We weren't raised the same. We had to really do the work to make us work.

The biggest mountain I had to climb was my very big spirit of independence. Even though I was married, I wasn't going to allow his doing or not doing to affect me. It was like I was always prepared for the other shoe to drop in a sense because I'd seen and felt this happen so many times. But when I started really praying about this matter, I allowed God to lead me, and honestly, through a lot of trial and error, we were blessed in a sense because we both fought and refused to give up on each other.

Harold, Jr. had a very loving example of marriage to model after. His parents are very wholesome people and a great example of love. They openly love each other and have a very kind, loving relationship. I was able to see that modeled- a loving marriage.

Initially, it created a lot of conflict. What Harold, Jr. saw and what I saw growing up was different. He didn't initially understand why I'd make decisions without consulting him, and it'd create conflict. He didn't feel respected as the head of the household, but I felt like I was not a child. There was a lot of conflict, and I was envious because he had a model family.

My mindset was, "You saw your parents honor each other. I saw men use my mom and throw her away." I assumed that's what he was going to do to me. I went into the marriage as I enjoyed it while it lasted because it's probably not going to last. It was almost a form of self-sabotage, and I really had to pray and work through my mindset led by childhood trauma.

Childhood trauma is funny. It can be the smallest details that make the biggest indentation in your heart. As I reflected on my views on marriage, I thought of the time when I was about seven years old and was spending the night at my aunt's house. In the middle of the night, my aunt packed me up, and we went on a stakeout to catch her husband cheating in the act. It was ingrained in me that men weren't faithful. The crazy part is that it was the most loving, best relationship and marriage I'd witnessed at that point, and even then, I saw my aunt being devalued and cheated on. That became my experience, and inadvertently, I believed it's acceptable for your husband to love you in that way because that's what I saw.

In retrospect, God sent me love, the example of love, and a parental example of love to help remold my heart. When I married Harold, Jr., I inherited great in-laws.

I call my father-in-law Father because he truly treats me like his daughter. It's a running joke that Harold, Jr. says to him, "I'm your son, she's your daughter-in-law." I do no wrong in his eyes. In the parental relationship, my mother-in-law is the disciplinarian for me. When Harold, Jr. and I would have our hardships in our relationship, my father-in-law would call and ask me how I was doing. I'd explain to him how he restored my love for my Heavenly Father because I experienced the love of an earthly father. He helped me to have a restored identity as a father, and that helped me. He taught me as a true father and helped me identify my different callings and gifts and fostered their growth.

He saw my strengths and weaknesses and stewarded them. Like a parent, he allowed me to grow in the grace of God but to steward it. He helped redirect my strong will and taught me how to use it for the greater good. For me, my spiritual parents really began to birth me, deal with areas that needed to be dealt with, and develop the areas. It was strengthening. They were understanding and loving as I healed and developed into a more mature woman spiritually and mentally.

Over the years, I learned to approach my marriage differently. When you approach it as we are building something that's going to last, a lot changes. I wanted something different than what I saw because what I saw was really messed up.

I had to allow myself to learn as I was exposed to these examples of love. They really exposed me to something different. Even as simple as eating dinner together and how to handle conflict. I would rather emulate that than what I experienced.

Subconsciously, we believe our love is performance-based and conditional; basically, if I don't do what you want me to do, then you won't love me. Even as I've gotten older and gained weight, I would wonder if my husband's love for me would expire because the conditions changed, but through love, I learned that's not how it works. Harold, Jr. loves my body even with extra weight. Even when I wasn't still 150 pounds, he told me I was the most beautiful woman he'd ever seen in his life.

I realized I had to fix the broken identity within myself to believe it truly, and that is a work in progress. A continuous work on myself to break down those broken things and rebuild stronger walls.

Harold, Jr. is a man of great patience, and through our almost 17 years of marriage, we've been through so many joys and pains. Over the years, Harold, Jr. has taught me the meaning of unconditional love. He has shown me a life that I never thought possible. He has made me see color again in a world that had become dark. Somehow, God created a person who was just what I needed.

He's not afraid to correct me and tell me no, and he's equally not too afraid to wrap me in his arms and love me even greater. He's a protector, a provider, a covering. He's my greatest intercessor. He prays for me and confirms my God-given purpose. He pushes me even when I don't want to be pushed, and he believes in me. He's the most brilliant mind that I have ever known.

He has the ability to visualize and create things like no one else that I know. I know that our connection on earth is much greater than us. I know that God joined us together to make a great impact on His Kingdom. He has filled a void in my life that only God could have led him to do.

Chapter 23

Praying for Hannah

It's true that love finds you when you least expect it. That was true of Harold, Jr. and of the way we grew our family.

Harold, Jr. and I had been married for five years. I was now in my 30s, working and we were raising AJ. Harold, Jr. had been pretty set on not having children, and while I honestly felt my biological clock ticking, my thoughts about having another baby were in the back of my head. I'd always wanted to have another daughter. It was something I'd asked God for and prayed about soon after I'yanna died, but we weren't trying, and we hadn't had a discussion about having a baby.

As a mom, you always want to heal your child's heart and I knew that AJ was hurting in ways even he didn't understand. His village poured into him as much as possible, but as his mom, I felt responsible for somehow filling that void. AJ longed for a sibling and healing his heart. It was apparent from his behavior that losing her had deeply affected him emotionally, and I dedicated a lot of time and energy to helping him try and heal from the heartbreak, even through my own heartbreak.

While we weren't planning to have a baby, the premonition of the blessings that were to abound became apparent when my father-in-law prophesied from the pulpit that I was going to have a baby. I was sitting in the front row of church one Sunday when he said, "Harold III is on his way."

I laughed out loud and joked about it. *Yeah, right, I was having a baby.* Like Sarah in the Bible, when she was told she was going to have a baby at the ripe old age of 90, I just didn't think it was feasible timing.

However, my laughter turned to concern when I realized my period was a whole week late. My body is like clockwork and always has been. For the fourth time in my life, I found myself nervously waiting on the results of a pregnancy test.

When I say I was utterly shocked when the test came back positive, my mouth was literally stuck hanging open! Every emotion went through me. I was laughing and crying at the same time. I was excited to have a child with the man I loved. We were in a good place, and for the first time, I felt really emotionally and physically ready to carry my child and create a stable, loving environment, complete with two present and mature parents, a spiritual foundation, financial stability, and a supportive village. This was truly what I'd dreamed of.

When my father-in-law prophesied it, I was already three weeks pregnant. He said he had a dream and he'd seen a boy. While I was excited to have a baby, I was scared because I knew I was having a boy when I desperately wanted a daughter.

The moment I could, I wanted to know the gender of the child growing in my womb. I knew I'd be happy if I had a boy, but God promised me I could raise a little girl.

My pregnancy was healthy and progressive, and everyone was extremely excited for us, especially the grandparents. Both my mom and Harold, Jr.'s parents were over the moon and spoiled me so much throughout my pregnancy. I'm talking phone calls, good meals, and lots of love and encouragement.

Deep down I was anxious to know the gender as soon as I could. The prophecy of a son, and the hope of a girl, were internally wearing on my heart. No matter the gender I'd cherish this baby and be the best mother I could be.

After that 13-week point, Harold, Jr. and I made an appointment with a local gender reveal boutique. Harold, Jr. picked me up on my lunch break at work so we could go to a baby sonogram shop called My Baby Bump in Sango.

I gazed out the window as he drove through town and we passed the same gas station where Adrian had given me the ultimatum about I'yanna. My heart dropped thinking about that day, losing I'yanna so tragically, but the moment I was experiencing going to learn the gender of my child with my husband.

It's a dizzying, whirlwind-type emotion in your head when you have a full-circle moment. I thanked God for my survival and the chance to experience the blessing of new motherhood again.

I was so nervous and scared as I entered My Baby Bump. I had butterflies because I knew the next few moments would change everything. I didn't say a word as the tech got me situated to do the ultrasound. She lifted my maroon sweater and adjusted my cream slacks to apply the jelly. I drank a lot of water before the appointment, but as the tech talked me through the process, she revealed I had a stubborn one who wouldn't move in the right direction so she could get the best angle to detect the gender. She took a few pictures, but they weren't great quality.

Disappointment began to set in.

"I think it's a girl," the tech said, moving the ultrasound fob across my round belly.

"A girl!" I repeated, staring at Harold, Jr., who was proudly watching the monitor. He looked into my eyes with joy, and I lost it.

I burst into tears, overcome with complete joy.

The tech was very confused and thought I was crying because I didn't want a girl. I explained through tears I was so happy because I wanted a girl!

The tech saw my joy and wanted to ensure she was giving the best information, so she asked us to schedule another appointment for the following week so she could take more pictures and make a more accurate final decision on the gender.

Although it had not been 100 percent confirmed, I felt in the depths of my soul that God had made good on his promise to me to be able to raise a little girl. The week could not go by fast enough, and when we returned, the same tech took more pictures and confirmed it was a girl! My joy abounded. We had believed God the first time, and that total confirmation was healing.

I was an emotional wreck as I realized God had given me a daughter again, and tears of joy overflowed again. Harold, Jr. and I shared our journey, explaining to the tech the loss of I'yanna and the desire to raise a daughter. I told her about the christening dress I'd saved. The tech was overcome with emotions, and we all wept tears of joy in the Baby Bump office. God is so faithful and good!

During my pregnancy, I experienced healing beyond my understanding. It felt truly like a second chance. Everything was aligned with God's will, and I was in a great place in life.

We knew what we were going to name her before she was born and had put great thought into her name. For years, I had carried her name in my wallet. I'd printed out the name, the origin, and the meaning, and I'd taped it in my wallet even before I got pregnant. I knew when I had a daughter, I would name her Hannah, after Hannah in the Bible.

Hannah was barren, and when she went to the sanctuary, she was so burdened she couldn't conceive. She appeared drunk to the high priest because she was so distraught and praying so deeply. That was me. I cried and prayed to the Lord, "Please let me have a daughter. I will give this baby back to you." I wasn't barren, but my desire to have a daughter ran deep. God delivered on his promise.

Hannah means favor and grace. Her grandma, Gwen, gave her middle name. She has the same initials as her dad. Keliah means fortress.

Hannah Keliah Browning was born July 24, 2013, at Tennova-Gateway Hospital in Clarksville, Tennessee. It was a new hospital that had been built on the north side of town, but it was the same hospital namesake that I'd birthed I'yanna at.

The same doctor who oversaw the birth of I'yanna oversaw the birth of Hannah.

Hannah was born special. She came out encased in her embryonic sac. We were told it was a rarity. Harold, Jr. said it was scary but amazing to witness. Although I had been induced, my water never broke. To me, it was symbolic that from the very beginning of her life, she was shielded and protected, and she was the child God had promised. The moment Hannah was placed in my arms she occupied a place in my heart that was made just for her. I loved her so much.

It was uncanny how much she looked like her father. Her chubby little cheeks, beautiful almond-shaped eyes, and puckered little lips. She didn't have any hair like my other babies, but she was so cute. She had all the extra folds and I fed her in all her chubbiness.

Having Hannah was so fulfilling because I had prayed so much for this child. It was such a full-circle moment. It was a moment in my journey of healing that I exhaled deeply. I would protect and fight fiercely for my daughter. It was a promise I silently made her, and I knew that her father, both earthly and heavenly, would also protect and love her just as diligently.

I learned not to be swayed when God has made you a promise. It's a realization that God's promises are "yes," and in him, Amen. He makes good on everything He promises.

As a newborn, all her sassiness and personality showed through. She may have physically looked like her father, but as I experienced her as a baby, a toddler, and a young child, Hannah possessed so many of my personality traits.

As a baby, she had colic really bad, but she was a good baby. She was so sweet. Hannah wasn't a toddler into a lot of stuff, and I didn't have any issues with her. I cherish so many firsts with Hannah that had been stolen from me with I'yanna, and for that, I truly and deeply cherished and had such deep gratitude in every moment.

Watching my daughter take her first steps, hearing her speak in full sentences, seeing her interact in church as the congregation baby, lose teeth, go to kindergarten, learn to tie her shoes, excel in school, and develop as a little human. I cherished the big and small moments. I was in love with her day-to-day life. I would literally stop in gratitude and thank God for giving me what I'd prayed so diligently for and allowing me to experience the full gamut of what love meant in marriage, parenthood, and my spiritual walk.

I didn't realize I needed healing, but watching my husband father his daughter has been something I never experienced. It touched my heart so deeply as I saw Hannah confidently rely on her father's love and have that reassurance that he's there to protect, support, and nurture her.

Harold, Jr., and Hannah are very close but have a different relationship than what she and I share. They have a very loving, affectionate relationship. She's truly his baby girl, and he would move mountains to ensure she is cared for and happy. They go on daddy/daughter dates, and since she was a baby, she finds comfort in laying on her dad's chest and going to sleep.

I didn't have that, and while sometimes I have to fight against pushing my own insecurities, I really pour into their relationship and encourage it. She has never experienced not being able to depend on her father. There's no *if* her dad can or *wants* to do something. She requests her father, and within his power, he will move heaven and Earth for his little girl. She has no doubt that her father will come through and she doesn't see his imperfections.

He's very loving, and it's been so refreshing and healing watching them. It helps me with my relationship with God. It helps me see what child-like faith is like. It helps me see that there's nothing your Heavenly Father won't do, especially if he says he is going to do it. God always shows up for you.

As I write this, my little girl is now ten years old. I kind of stay in my feelings about my kids growing up. I feel like I blinked, and she grew up. I have so many photos of her. I wished I'd done more with I'yanna, taken more photos and videos, and held on to more memories. I documented Hannah's life, holding on to and cherishing each stage of being her mom.

Hannah is like my little best friend. Raising her has been such a blessing. She's wise beyond her years and, even as a toddler, was such a sweet, little old soul. She's been a joy to raise although we haven't quite reached the teen years.

She dreams often and vividly, like her grandfather, Harold, Sr. She's such a great kid!

Hannah, like me, needs to know why, and she needs an answer. She will seek understanding. She likes things a certain way and can be a bit of a perfectionist. She wants to figure things out on her own. She loves her family and is a nurturer who loves to be a helper. She's funny, witty, and sweet.

Like me, she's opinionated, a bit sarcastic, and affectionate on her own terms. Once she's made up her mind, there's no changing it. She's very strong-willed.

Hannah is very ladylike and dainty. She's also very intelligent, persistent, and works hard for what she wants. As she continues to grow, I see so much of myself in her.

I won't lie, I spoil Hannah, and I know I'm the problem. I mean, at ten, I've equipped her with an iPhone and Apple watch, and yes, the latest craze right now is a $50 Stanley

Cup, and I got her one. Ole' girl is legit walking around with thousands of dollars' worth of accessories.

She's extremely fashionable because we both have a sneaker addiction. I thought I had a shopping problem with I'yanna, but now I've had years to really perfect it with Hannah. She stays sharp and I want her to be confident and know she's loved for exactly who she is. Though I'm the problem and spoil her, I would not have it any other way.

It's healed my heart to be able to do simple things together like dress alike, go to the salon and get our hair styled, get our nails done, and go on Starbucks runs. Even feeling her arms wrap around me for a hug is healing to my soul. I know it may be small things, but I cherish it so much because each experience has glued a little piece of my once shattered heart back together.

My son has my DNA, but there are certain things I couldn't pass down to him, so to raise and rear and have the ability to have a mini-me has been fun and exciting. It's also a greater responsibility and has put me on task to be a better woman.

I know she's watching and mimicking her mom. I want to show her so much, and much like my mom, Anna, I don't want her to go through the traumas and pains I went through as I learned the hard knocks in life. I know life won't be perfect for Hannah, but I want her to feel at least prepared and have a deep relationship with God so she can face anything that comes her way.

It's a beautiful feeling to get the full experience of something that felt like it had been snatched away from me for so long. I still grieve and miss I'yanna and I want to keep her legacy alive always.

One gift I'd like to one day give Hannah is my story. Right now, she's too young, and there are parts of my life I want to protect her from because they just aren't age-appropriate. I've shared pieces of my story, even parts of this book, with her, and we've started to have small conversations.

But Hannah doesn't press me. She has the wisdom to know that in time, she will know more. Certain portions are still very painful, and one day, I know we will talk. I will share my experiences and pains in hopes of helping her avoid those painful life lessons. I hope she doesn't judge me but sees the path of growth and knows my undying and unconditional love for my children.

I prayed for Hannah, and I have so much I pray about for Hannah. Like AJ, I pray about Hannah every day.

I pray she's comfortable being her authentic self, is solidified in her purpose, and knows her worth. I want her to be confident in who she is and who God called her to be. I want her to be content with how God created her.

I was always unsure of my calling, purpose, and destiny. I want her to be sure of her calling, purpose, and destiny and secure with how God orchestrated her. My prayer is often that her innocence is protected and that things are not revealed before their timing. I pray that she's a leader and has the courage and tenacity to lead and not have to follow.

Hannah has been such a healing addition to our family, and it was so healing for me to see AJ have a sibling again and see that relationship blossom. They have such a normal brother/sister bond even with their 11-year age gap.

It wasn't the picture of family perfection. Initially, when Hannah was a baby, AJ was really good with her and would help out. He took on that big brother role, but when she turned four or five years old, they did not get along at all. AJ had been the only child for a while and would feel slighted, and they would argue.

But as AJ matured, so did his outlook on his baby sister. He now picks her up from school and takes her to get snacks and treats. Her dad does, too. She told me she likes when Dad and AJ pick her up because she usually gets to stop and get a nice treat. She kind of has them wrapped around her finger. It's his way of bonding with her and showing his love.

One thing that has not changed about me is what I said and felt the day I was at the gas station. I knew I would not abort my baby, being a mom will always be a top priority in my life.

Hannah is my physical reminder of the promise God made to me. I thought about the day I buried I'yanna and my obsession with her dress. Then I think about the dress I saved from her christening with faith I'd see my second baby girl wear it one day. And it was a full circle, amazing moment when we christened Hannah in her sister's dress.

I think about the dresses of the future with Hannah. Her prom dress. Her wedding dress. I think of the hopes and dreams of my daughter and the blessing it is to be here and experience each one with her as she grows into a beautiful woman of God.

Chapter 24

December's Sorrow

My phone alarm blared in my ear and as I rolled over and turned it off, the date, not the time, caught my eye.

December 7, 2020.

My mind went immediately to I'yanna.

I laid in bed not snoozing. I was wide awake as the date made my heart drop. I knew I needed to get up and get dressed for my commute to my downstairs home office, but I felt stuck for a moment.

December 7th always awakened a fresh feeling of aching grief in my heart. I could still remember every moment of that last day I spent with I'yanna like it just happened.

My thoughts wandered to what it'd be like now. She'd be 13 years old now. I wonder how she'd look. Would she look like me? She'd favored me as a baby with her fair skin, head full of hair, and a big smile. I had so many unanswered questions

Would she and Hannah be close like the relationship I had with my sisters?

Would she have been funny and sarcastic or sweet and quiet?

Would she and her brother AJ be besties or have that little sister, big brother annoyance but love like Hannah and AJ?

Would she be on TikTok dancing like the other teens or going through the woes of puberty?

Would she have the girly, girly fashion I often dressed her in as an infant or be a tomboy?

Would she be team natural with that thick curly hair or be dying to wear it straight?

I tried to paint a picture of what she would have looked like, but my canvas always felt kind of blank, a void like the reality I usually felt whenever I thought about my baby girl. All the what-ifs and scenarios flood my mind heavily on December 7th.

It was like this every year, but I often thought and dreamed about I'yanna many days. Sometimes she was still forever 7-months-old, and I imagined her soft skin and her infectious smile. Other times I tried to create a likeness of her in my mind. She would be older, in high school. I didn't want to forget her. Her memory was something I treasured.

Not being able to see your child grow up after all the love you've committed to them is a cruel feeling that leaves you longing forever to give love and receive love from them. The ache that never left my heart took a front seat, center stage with such intensity.

"Mommy!" Hannah's voice yelled after her little knock.

"Yes," I yelled back through the closed door.

"It's almost time for me to log in to school."

"Ok, I'll be right there," I said.

We'd opted to enroll Hannah in the virtual academy since COVID-19 kidnapped the entire year of 2020 and held it for ransom.

Virtual school during the COVID-19 pandemic had taken a toll on all of us 30-something parents who hadn't even seen a math book in 15-20 years. The memes on social media pictured us parents losing our crap, crying, just taken aback by our new unqualified roles as teachers. We were all questioning our intelligence and sanity by this point.

Hannah was a smart girl who had adjusted well. I felt bad for AJ. It was his senior year in high school, and what was supposed to be a memorable year was being bullied by the pandemic. Prom, graduation, and senior activities were all up in the air and pending for 2021, depending on how many more people died.

It truly felt like we were living in the Twilight Zone. When we ventured out in public for necessities, we all looked like lost masked aliens.

On The Wings of Grace

I was happy AJ got to play basketball with the school team this year. "*#25!* That's my baby!" I often yelled as he ran up and down the court. I was the clapping mom screaming for her son through her mask as everyone sat socially distanced in the bleachers. Proud was an understatement, and nobody was going to tell me that I couldn't root for my baby.

I had such a busy day ahead of me. It was nearing Christmas, and we were working on three closings just this week. I needed to get up. I was tired but held so much passion in my niche of helping people find their foundation, their nest, their place to build. Homes had to be bought and sold, and I was the middle woman. While my mind told me to get up and get dressed, my heart was elsewhere as I lay watching the ceiling fan rotate slowly.

I could feel Iyanna's soft black curls against my cheek again. I could feel her warm, sweet, milky breath on my neck as I rocked her to sleep. Her little mouth hung open, and those fat rosy cheeks just hugged her face.

I'd watch her sleep, gazing at her innocently, wondering the same questions I had today: who would this sweet little girl be? What would I teach her? I imagined her small feet in my hand, her soft skin, and her small baby rolls. I could almost feel her in my arms again. I just wanted to hang on to every memory I had of her.

In 13 years, I'd healed in many ways, but the longing for my child had not weakened a bit.

I wish Hannah could've met her. I wish she would've known the love of a father like Harold, Jr. I wish she could celebrate with us as AJ graduates from high school this year. I wish she'd be opening presents with us on Christmas, wearing matching pajamas like the suburban families do. I just wished so hard, and the what-ifs and if-onlys followed on its heels.

Why'd he have to kill my baby? Why didn't he just commit suicide and spare her? She didn't deserve that. Before I knew it a few tears escaped and spilled down my cheeks.

"Oh I'yanna..."

No matter how much time passes and how far I've come in my healing, I still have the days when it all just hurts my heart so badly.

In the year of COVID-19, it was the first time I hadn't been able to memorialize her publicly and just speak her name and release balloons or a butterfly. She was one of the youngest names in the Butterfly Memorial Garden, where I'd spoken in front of other grieving parents whose children had been murdered.

It was the first time in 13 years that I couldn't hang an ornament bearing her sweet face on the large Christmas tree in the Montgomery County Library. Or say her name in front of hundreds of other grieving families who, if they could, have one Christmas wish, to have their loved one back and not be a part of this community club full of tragedy and pain.

I never wanted anyone to forget I'yanna. She was mine for seven months but lived forever in my heart. She mattered then and still does today.

The overwhelming feelings quickly led me into a prayer to work through the emotional dip that had overtaken me. I spoke to my Father, leaning deep into thanksgiving and supplication, just thanking him for I'yanna. I thanked Him for growth, grace and love, my family and blessings, endurance, overcoming, and his love and healing.

My lips were moving, and tears rolled down my face as my prayer visited December 7, 2007, again and again. Mentally traveling through the winds of my life's ups and downs. Like the prayer of Hannah, my beautiful daughter's namesake, it became incoherent and filled with emotion as I supplicated for strength, wisdom, and perseverance. "God, I need you," I say quietly, and I get lost in my emotions as I open my heart and let out what I was holding in.

I felt free and heard by my Father as I lay in bed with my eyes closed, praying, and crying on December 7th. When people ask me how I've made it through such tragedy, all glory goes to God because in moments like this, I feel him the most.

As I lay still in my silent prayer, I felt a hand on my hand. I knew it was Harold, Jr. It made me cry harder. He's such a godsend and part of my healing. He kneeled on my side of the bed and held my hand as I prayed.

He knew this day hit me hard no matter how strong-willed and determined I was. Although he met me after I'yanna died, he'd seen me on my toughest days. Harold, Jr. has always had a place for me to heal in his arms. He was gentle when it came to I'yanna. He was a spiritual source of comfort.

When my prayer ended, I looked at him through watery eyes and smiled. "Amen, Mrs. Browning," he said, returning the smile. "Amen. You got this, babe." He kissed my hand.

"Mommy!" Hannah's voice rang out again. "It's time for me to log in for Zoom!"

"I got it, babe," Harold, Jr. said, getting up and going to assist Hannah.

I heard their playful banter in the hallway and Hannah's laugh. Their relationship was so sweet. It's what I dreamed of as a child. She was a daddy's girl.

Ping. Another email. I looked at my phone quickly as I stood up. A lender.

Ping. A client.

Business never stops – even when you're grieving. I had a lot of business to handle. I typed on my phone as I walked towards the restroom to shower and get dressed. The hustle and bustle of a day in the Browning's home had begun.

When I sat down in my home office in the basement, my mug of hot coffee straight from the Keurig gave me the kick of caffeine I needed to get through the busy crazy day.

To be honest, there wasn't much time to stop and think or grieve. Nor did I want to stay in that place of sorrow all day. I always wanted to celebrate I'yanna's life and remember that she lived, and not how she died.

Phone calls, email after email, texting, and juggling so many things at a time were my norm. Hannah had moved to the office with me after her first online class and sat at her little desk with her headphones on, doing schoolwork.

Text messages flooded my phone with a mass of *thinking of you* sentiments, notes about Iyanna's memory, home closing conversations and business details. At lunch I logged onto Facebook to post a business post.

When I'yanna died Facebook had been a newer concept. Facebook had finally become open to non-college students and had increased greatly in popularity in 2007.

Social media is a huge deal now, where you can do business, market, sell, and brand, maintain personal connections and create analytics about it all. I had over 2,000 friends somehow. Connections in the community happened daily, and most of them didn't even know me when I had I'yanna. Some know nothing about her tragic demise, or maybe everyone knows.

The Facebook memory hit me as soon as I logged in and a photo of I'yanna from a tribute I'd made in years past stared back at me. I thought about the day the photo was taken. Just an ordinary day in our life before everything changed.

I created a new post and shared one of the few photos I had of her. She was sleeping on the couch. Her pink onesie looked cozy as she slumbered. She had that head of lush jet-black hair that was full of semi-curly soft hair. She was a beautiful baby!

"Today marks 13 long years that I've lived without you... much has changed in life, but the consistent thing is your mom misses you terribly... it's a big year for us... every celebration reminds me that we have one piece missing. Love you, Baby!"

The post quickly garnered over 200 likes and dozens of comments. It felt good to remember and say her name and for everyone to think of her life.

I redirected and shared Harold, Jr.'s business post after his 8 a.m. meeting. It was a photo of our latest homeowners! We got them closed and in a home.

Later that night, when all was quiet, I lay in bed next to Harold, Jr. and read through some of the Facebook comments and text messages on my phone. Each one was sweet and heartfelt.

One of my friends said I was the strongest person she knew. I felt honored, but honestly, I thought about times I wasn't strong and was broken.

If people only knew my entire story, I thought to myself.

Fairlen of 2020 was a sophisticated businesswoman who always kept her hair and nails done, traveled with her family, and handled her business. She loved her family and loved God. That's what those 2,000 plus Facebook friends could take from my social media profile. While on the surface that's true, it had been a jagged, bumpy, curvy road I walked barefoot and broken to get to where I was.

I scrolled further down my page and laughed, showing Harold, Jr. the photo I'd posted of Hannah's praise dancing at our church.

"Our baby was killing it, wasn't she?" I said laughing out loud, "Look at the intensity on her face."

Harold, Jr. laughed, "That's my baby girl. You know her grandparents were too proud!"

"You know, I know!" I said.

I scrolled up to a picture of AJ playing basketball with his school team. We were overjoyed that virtual schools could still play for their school. I'm nervous knowing COVID-19 can spread among teams, but I couldn't say no to another thing and ruin his senior year any further. I couldn't believe he'd be graduating in a few months.

I was deeply in my mom-feelings anytime I thought about how much my baby boy was growing up. I cried when he took his senior photos. He'd been my ride or die through it all, and if anyone else felt that pain head-on like I did, it was him.

He was so young when she died but he definitely remembers that time he was five years old and the man he thought was his friend took his little sister from him. I'd worried about AJ for years, but I could be nothing short of extremely proud of the man my baby had grown into.

Man... that word made my stomach drop. He was going to college next year. He was leaving. He was probably going to be moving out. He was going to be a... man. For some reason the thought of another child leaving me just made me feel ill.

I turned the phone alarm on, put it on the charger and put it on my nightstand. I could feel Harold, Jr. staring at me watching my every movement. I flipped to face him.

"What!?" I asked, my eyes questioning his stare.

"You good?" He asked.

"Yeah, I'm good," I said.

"You want to talk?" He asked.

"I think I'm OK," I replied. "This is always a tough day. I feel like if I just stay busy, I'm not going think about it a lot. But I sure wish you could've met 'Yanna. She was sweet. She would've loved you as a stepdad."

"I would've loved her, too. In fact, I do love her because she's a part of you," He said.

I smiled.

He was so sweet and cheesy, and I loved it.

We talked about Hannah. I asked when he thought we should tell her about I'yanna. She was just six years old and too young to understand. I wanted her to hold on to that innocence and just be my baby for as long as she could. Maybe I'd tell her in pieces. Tell her that she had a sister and what eventually happened. When was the right time? Ten years old, 12-years-old, 15-years-old? We both decided we'd know when it was the right time for her.

She'd seen pictures and I'd been vague that it was a sweet baby no longer with us, but she didn't know the gore and grim behind her sister's death.

I didn't want her life to be bookmarked by the murder of a sibling. One day I'd tell her everything. One day I'd share my entire story with her and hopefully she will learn from my mistakes and we will break the generational curses of teen pregnancy, self-esteem issues, daddy issues and more.

I had to get it right for Hannah and I was working my hardest and sopping up every minute with my growing baby.

She'd healed me in many ways by restoring the love in my heart for a daughter. She'd brought something beyond special to my heart. Hannah was my prayer after all I'd been through.

Harold, Jr. held me, and I tried to sleep.

I really worked on quieting my mind, but everything rolled through my brain as I shut my eyes. I could see his face, her grave, the "Angel's kiss" on her cheek.

My eyes would open.

I'd close my eyes. I'd see Hannah praise dancing and then my friend praise dancing at I'yanna's funeral. The music, the pink casket.

My eyes opened.

"Please quiet my mind, God," I prayed.

The peace that God had always given when I asked settled on my heart and I was able to settle into my tired soul. I was exhausted from the day, but overall, I felt blessed and cared for.

In all I'd faced, I was glad to be alive to continue my journey and honor my baby on another December 7th.

Chapter 25

Walking in My Purpose

Throughout my healing journey, helping people has always given me the greatest joy. Whether it's through my job, sharing my story with a grieving mother, or pouring into someone spiritually, I've truly experienced firsthand the blessings and joy of giving. And through this journey, I've discovered why giving is much better than receiving. Giving has turned out to be therapeutic and beneficial to my journey.

But I always struggled with my purpose. What was I born to do? What was I supposed to be doing? I got my answer the day of I'yanna's funeral, but it would be some time before I felt worthy enough to walk in that purpose.

Harold, Sr., my dad, my father-in-law said to me on the day of I'yanna's funeral, "Now it's time for you to walk in your ministry." I heard him, but I knew I needed time, growth, and healing. He never let up on what he said to me.

Momma gave me life, but Harold, Sr. gave birth to me spiritually. I'm the product of my spiritual father. He wasn't playing games with me and still doesn't. He literally took me under his wing and taught me the power of the Bible. No one would have been able to tell me that this tragedy would have led me here.

I'd always had the gift of gab. Growing up, I was always told I was wise beyond my years. I was kind of an old soul and hung out with my grandma and older people. I never hung out with people my own age. Growing up, kids would be on the playground, and I'd be sitting with my grandma and her friends. Some kids watched cartoons. I watched *Heat of the Night* with my grandma.

I was just always wise beyond my years and always had something to say. I always had to have the last word. Harold, Sr. pulled that quality out of me and taught me how to use it to help others. He tasked me to be a student of the Bible and how to delve into and meditate on it.

I'd never thought about preaching, being an elder or teaching in the church. My father, Harold, Sr., saw what I couldn't see. He really encouraged me. He studies to study, not just to preach. He taught me how to study and research in the Bible, how to examine text, to ask questions, break down the text, and background to get a deeper meaning of it.

I learned how to examine the figure of speech, word origins, and the historical and literary context of Bible passages. I took the nosiness in me and learned to research and understand the deeper meaning of the scriptures.

This has helped me grow spiritually because I needed a deeper and greater understanding of my own personal journey. God always has a plan, and we're never fully aware of all the details until we need them.

The Bible became alive to me, a living, moving organism. It's not just words on paper for me. Understanding allows you to take a front seat to the Word, and it becomes alive and not just a secondhand account. To feel, see, and experience the Word of God has been the greatest gift.

I didn't set out to be a preacher and didn't know one day I would be doing it. My dad gave me an assignment that I had to preach, and I couldn't tell him no. I went through developmental training, which was a college-level class.

The first time I got up to preach was in 2009. That first Sunday after preaching, Harold, Sr. called me into his office. He lovingly said, 'Fairlen, you're trying to separate yourself from the Word you have to minister. You can't. You have to minister from a place in you. You are who God has called you to be."

I was struggling a little, and he explained to me that I couldn't be separated from my message. I have to be the first recipient and partaker of the Word that God has given to me. He didn't want me to preach at people, but first preach to myself and then feed the people. I was an expounder. After that, I learned to minister from a place of realness—from a genuine place in my heart.

One of the most impactful and personal messages I ministered was about the woman at the well. Christianity has dubbed this woman a loose harlot, but I identified with her so much. Society said this woman had five husbands and was living with a man who wasn't hers. When you go back and really study the text, you are reminded that back then, a wife couldn't divorce a man; a man had to divorce her. Those marriages were often arranged when they were young.

We don't really know the true details of why she had five husbands. It could've been that she was young and outlived five husbands. The younger brother often married the deceased brother's wife. Maybe she was a product of her environment. Maybe because what had happened to her caused her to choose a life not well-received. We don't know.

But what we do know is she went to the well by herself at noon, the most inconvenient time for most, but convenient for her. She went at that time so that she wouldn't have to deal with people ostracizing her... whispering. She went to this well by herself to escape her reality. To be alone.

However, what she didn't know was that Jesus chose a special route that day to be with her. He was determined that he must go through Samaria. The Jews and Samaritans had a hostile relationship. They would usually go around Samaritans, but Jesus was adamant about going through Samaria—just to encounter this woman at this well. He sent his disciples to go get food to ensure he'd have time to be alone with this woman. He had a divine appointment with this woman.

Jesus asked her for water. She was shocked at why he, this Jew, would ask her for water. She understood her place. She knew who she was. She'd accepted what people had thought about her. She understood she was a promiscuous woman and practically forbade Jesus from speaking to her. Furthermore, she was drawing water at noon, during the hottest hour of the day, when most would usually draw their water in the morning before the sun would be too high. Jesus had a plan, just for her. Many of us know the rest of the story, and Jesus wanted to give her a gift that even through her tragedies in life, he wanted her to know that she was still blessed.

I often felt like the woman at the well. There were so many things I disassociated myself from because of what people knew about my past. All the hurtful things said about me. Blaming me, saying that I had pushed Lionel to do the unthinkable act he'd done, to take my daughter's life and then his own. I didn't push him to do that and there was nothing I did that required him to react that way. I didn't have a covenant with him. No one will ever understand why he did what he did. But God knows. People have, and will continue to, created a narrative about me to help them *justify* things they will never be able to understand.

However, like that woman at the well, I carried so much shame and it held me back from preaching and teaching because I didn't feel qualified. But God took an unusual route just to meet me at the well to reveal purpose.

The Enemy would make me feel like it was my fault and tell me I would never be good enough to help anyone. I was the woman at the well. I'd go to church and sit in the back. I didn't have any friends, and I didn't want to be confronted with my past. God had to confront me about my past.

Jesus had to confront me and say to me, "Yes, this bad thing happened, but what are you going to do with it? I can still use it for your good. The Word is still the Word. All things work together for those who love the Lord and are called to his purpose."

God knew it all. He knew every mistake I was going to make. He knew the tragedy that would befall me. But all in all, he always had a plan to use me. The purpose isn't always understandable, especially one like mine.

Though we may detour in life, our purpose will always be fulfilled. While I walked in my purpose spiritually, I also found purpose in natural life.

What Harold, Sr. spoke over me during a time I couldn't understand helped me eventually understand the way God designed me to be and not the way the world wants me to be. I've learned to be myself genuinely. I think one of the greatest things God was able to teach me was how to be delivered from people's opinions.

All along, God wanted and needed to use me. My story is what God used to put me in a position to be a good representative of the kingdom.

Like the woman at the well, I have my flaws and past mistakes, but I have to say they happened, and now what? God delivered me, and now there is work to do.

My purpose and mission is to be impactful. I want to be impactful for the kingdom and really make disciples and enlarge the kingdom. I want to be effective. I'm most impacted when I see people come to the realization of their ability and understanding that we all have a purpose, no matter what we have to or had to go through to get to it.

I'yanna was a part of my purpose. There are days that I still struggle with why it had to be that way, but some things I learned to stop trying to figure out. But what I do know is that through sharing her story, and keeping her alive, and honoring her, I'm walking in my purpose. When I do that, I feel her life isn't in vain.

Chapter 26

God's Grace

February 2023

I couldn't go to sleep. The excitement from my 40th birthday bash was still running through me like a rushing current and had me in a euphoric state of total bliss. I was still smiling from ear to ear.

The rain pitter-pattered on my bedroom window. I thought the mucky weather would keep the guests away. I had been so nervous as the party's start neared. Harold, Jr. and I had put so much time and money into making this night special, and it had been a massive undertaking. We'd hired a party planner to turn my vision into a reality. Despite all that went into inviting the 80-100 guests, I kept picturing just a handful of people showing up.

I texted Harold, Jr., "Did anyone show up?" As the cocktail hour was going into full swing.

I waited anxiously for his reply. "We've run out of seats. It's so full!" Harold, Jr. had replied.

At that moment, a realization hit me. All my life, people would look at me, Fairlen, and notice a vibrant social circle, but even surrounded by people, I didn't always feel like people liked me. I often felt like a loner and had become self-conscious and analytical about my relationships and how people viewed me.

People who know me may be shocked to learn that although I'm naturally outgoing and bubbly, I'm also an overthinker and over worrier.

The moment I walked into the room, all the thinking and worrying disappeared and were replaced by adrenaline and joy. Everyone clapped and cheered. A feeling of great comfort enveloped me, and it was beautiful to have so many familiar faces in the room celebrating a joyous occasion rather than one of somberness. My life has come a long way.

Family, friends, my church family, and co-workers had traveled from near and far to attend. I felt so grateful for each and every person in the room who had contributed in some way to the woman I'd become over the past four decades. Many had seen me at my absolute worst and watched as I emerged from the darkness. I truly felt their joy in this celebration of my life.

Turning 40 was definitely a milestone, and while I'd gone back and forth about having a party, I was so glad I'd been talked into it. It was a grand affair! It was everything I could imagine and moments from the night played in my head like a cinematic movie. I kept reliving the highlights.

The swanky Nashville ballroom was decorated with diamond centerpieces that towered over linens. Fancy chandeliers dangled overhead. It was a whole vibe. A huge '40' was lit up on the stage and life-size cut-outs of me were around the room. A hip-hop violinist performed classic hits to our excited cheers. A live band had the energy and mood flowing, and we danced until I had to pull my red-bottom heels off and line dance barefoot.

We had a time that night! It was truly a celebration, and we looked good doing it as everyone had shown up in their fancy dresses for the elegant all-black cocktail dinner.

I looked at pictures on my phone from the night, laughing and reliving the moments. I was tempted to wake

Harold, Jr. up and talk, but he was sleeping peacefully next to me, and I didn't want to disturb him. We were both tired from all the planning and moving pieces of the day.

Pictures captured the sentimental moments of the night, and I was welling up with tears again. I had figuratively and physically received my *flowers* and it was overwhelmingly emotional in a good way. Words professing admiration, inspiration, and pure love were showered on me and I, not a public crier, could not hold back the tears of joy and humility. I felt loved and beyond blessed.

I never should've made it to 40, I thought. There had been so many situations that the Enemy put in place to destroy me totally. It was nothing but the grace of God that kept me standing firm and moving forward at times when I'd wanted to quit.

I had a small revelation lying in bed after my party: I was exactly where I'd always dreamed of being and had been blessed with so many things I'd always prayed for. Pure gratitude encircled my entire heart, and I hugged it warmly.

I, Fairlen Browning, had lived through the most devastating loss and tragedy, found my purpose and calling, turned my life around, built a beautiful family with a man I loved, found joy in my career, strengthened my hope, and experienced redemption all by the grace of God.

It was God who helped me reach 40, and I could do nothing but thank God at that very moment. Only He knew all I'd been through to get to such a place of contentment and a mindset to appreciate both the tribulations and the blessings while still walking this journey called life.

My life has not been easy. I'd made a lot of bad decisions and experienced a lot of loss, especially in my young adulthood. At just 24 years old my entire life came to a complete halt as I was forced to deal with what can only be described as a horrific nightmare when I'yanna was stolen from me in such a violent way.

While I try to explain what happened, there are really no words that describe what living through a tragedy like that does to you and feels like. Time continues and you experience the throes of grief in a series of moments and emotions. It's a forced journey of discovery and it's bumpy, scary, unfamiliar terrain. But I'm still walking and still standing.

Losing I'yanna broke me and saved me. I was living a toxic and reckless existence, and her death stopped the trajectory I was on to self-sabotage and eventually self-destruct. Sharing her story and her memory has been a goal I've worked on for over a decade.

The kinds of relationships I had with men in my life had caused me so much heartbreak and pain. Abandonment, infidelity, and divorce were my common experiences, and having real, unconditional love was not something I thought was attainable. My heart has been broken so many times. My struggles had led me on a path that I knew I had to grow from and overcome. I'd found Harold, Jr., who wasn't perfect but was perfect for me.

I was once a hopeless person, but my faith and walk with God helped establish my hope.

I felt so much grace from God because where I'd been in life was not how I'd ended up. It was only Him who had helped me change and have the courage and ambition to progress beyond the pains in my life. There was nothing but gratitude and love for God in my heart for each and every blessing I'd ever received.

All my tests in life had truly become my testimony and at 40, I felt a true sense of redemption.

"To God be the glory!" I say out loud.

Reflecting over 40 years of life, I'd said during my party, "God has always seen about me. No matter where I've been in life, even when I didn't understand it or know how he's going to do it, He's really seen about me."

As I drifted to sleep, my heart was filled with complete peace. And there I floated away on God's wings of grace.

Fairlen Browning

www.ingramcontent.com/pod-product-compliance
Lightning Source LLC
Chambersburg PA
CBHW070945180426
43194CB00040B/947